CHRISTMAS ROSES AND OTHER STORIES

BY

ANNE DOUGLAS SEDGWICK

Christmas Roses

I

THEY were coming up everywhere in their sheltered corner on the wall-border, between the laurustinus and the yew hedge. She had always loved to watch their manner of emerging from the wintry ground: neck first, arched and stubborn; heads bent down as if with held breath and thrusting effort; the pale, bowed, folded flower, when finally it rose, still earthy, still part, as it were, of the cold and dark from which it came; so that to find them, as on this morning, clear, white, triumphant, all open to the wind and snow, was to renew the sense of the miraculous that, more than any other flower, they always gave her. More than any other flower, they seemed to mean to come, to will and compass it by the force of their own mysterious life. More than any other flower, winter piled upon their heads, unallured by spring and the promise of sunlight, they seemed to come from the pressure of a gift to bring rather than a life to seek. She thought always, when she saw them, of Christmas bells over snowy fields, in bygone centuries; of the Star in the East, and of the manger at Bethlehem. They were as ancient as that tradition, austere and immaculate witnesses in an unresponsive world; yet they were young and new, always; always a surprise, and even to her, old as she was, bereft and sorrowful, a reminder that life was forever a thing of births, of gifts, of miracles.

They did not fail her this morning when she came out to them, and she thought, as she stopped to look at them, that one was not really old when, in the shock of sheer happiness, one knew childhood again and its wonder. Yet, as she worked among them, cutting away dead leaves and adjusting sprays of evergreen so that the rains should not splash them with mud, it was a new analogy they brought; and, for the first time, measuring her resource after the appeal Tim's letter had made upon it, she reflected that the Christmas roses were rather like herself. She, too, in this wintry season of her life, was still determined and indomitable. Widowed and childless, with many mournings in her heart, griefs and devastations in her memory, she, too, was a force, silent and patient; and it was this that people still found in her. For the appeal always brought the answer. She had felt herself, so often, benumbed into lethargy, and, yielding to the mere mute instinct of self-preservation, had so often folded herself up and lapsed into the blank darkness of her grief (her husband's death, so many years ago; and Miles's, and little Hugh's, and her dear, dear Peggy's). But it had always been to hear herself, as if in a dream, called to from the outside world, and to feel herself, in answer, coming up again, rising, if only to snows and tempests, in a renewal of life which brought with it, always, a renewal of joy in life.

For months now, since August, she had been sunken in the last grief—it must be—that could come to her; for Miles was the last, of her own, who had remained—Peggy's youngest boy. The oldest, already a soldier, had been killed in the first months of the war, and, after all his years of peril, it had seemed as if Miles was to escape. But, cruelly, just at the turning of the tide, when victory had become assured, he had been shot down, and in his crashing fall through the air she had felt the end of everything, Peggy dying again with him; for Peggy, too, had died like that, crashing and falling and dragged, in a horrible hunting accident. There seemed, now, nothing more left to suffer, and nothing more to live for, either, unless it were her poor Tim; and it had, exactly, been Tim's letter that had driven her out to wrestle with the elements, after her wont in any disturbance or perplexity, so that she could think over what he told her while she wielded her trowel and fork on the convenient wall-border.

She had, on rising from the breakfast-table, sent Tim a wire: "I shall expect her. Writing later," and had then called to Parton to bring her old warm coat, her hood with its satin lining, and her buckled galoshes.

Parton was accustomed to her mistress's vagaries in regard to gardening, and made no comment on the enterprise except to express the hope that it would not snow again. Parton, in spite of her youth a most efficient combination of parlourmaid and lady's-maid, was devoted to her mistress; the little pat and tweak she gave to the bow of the hood, and the gentleness with which she adjusted the galoshes, expressed a close yet almost reverential relationship.

It was not freezing, and under the light fall of snow the ground was soft. Mrs. Delafield found herself enjoying the morning freshness as she tidied and weeded, and had her usual affectionate eye for the bullfinches nipping away at her plum-buds and the tits and robins at the little table spread with scraps for them near the house; while all the time Tim's letter weighed on her, and the problem it presented; and as she pondered on it, and on Rhoda, her niece, Tim's only child, her firm, square, handsome, old, white face was not devoid of a certain grimness.

Mrs. Delafield was very handsome, perhaps more handsome now than she had been in youth. Her brow, with the peak of thick white hair descending upon it, her thick black eyebrows and her rather thick, projecting nose, were commanding—almost alarmingly so to those who in her presence had cause for alarm. The merely shy were swiftly reassured by something merry in her gaze and by the benevolent grace still lingering on her firm, small lips. She had square eyes clearly drawn, and with an oddity in their mountain-brook colouring, for one was brown and one was freaked with grey. Her form was ample and upright, and in all her gestures there was swiftness and decision.

It was of Tim she thought at first, rather than of Rhoda, the cause of all their distresses. But she was not seeing Tim as he now existed, bleached, after his years of India, invalided, fretted by family cares, plaintive and pitiful. She saw him as a very little boy in their distant Northern nursery of sixty years ago, with bright curls, ruddy cheeks, and the blue eyes, candid and trusting, that he still kept; standing there, bare-armed and bare-legged, in his stiff, funny little dress of plaid, before the fire-guard, while nurse, irate, benevolent figure, cut bread and butter for breakfast. Dear little Tim! still her younger brother; still turning to her, as he had always done, for counsel or succour in any stress or anxiety. It was nothing new that the anxiety should be about Rhoda; there was nothing, even, that had surprised her in Tim's letter; yet she knew from the sense of urgency and even breathlessness within her that the blow which had been dealt him could not leave her unaffected. She could, after all, still suffer in Tim's suffering. And even before she had let her thoughts dwell decisively on Rhoda, she had found herself thinking, while the grimness settled on her face, "I shall know how to talk to her."

She had always known how to talk to the moody young beauty; that was why Tim had sent off this letter of desperate appeal. She never quite saw why Rhoda had not, from the first, felt in her merely an echo of her father's commonplace conventionality and discounted her as that. Rhoda had never, she felt sure, guessed how far from conventional she was; how much at heart, in spite of a life that had never left appointed paths, she knew herself to be a rebel and a sceptic; no one had ever guessed it. But there had always been between her and Rhoda an intuitive understanding; and that Rhoda from the first had listened and, from the first, had sometimes yielded, proved that she was intelligent.

Mrs. Delafield saw herself so accurately as Rhoda must see her. The terse, old-fashioned aunt in the country residence—yes, dear Fernleigh, square and mid-Victorian, with its name, and its creepers, its conservatory, and its shrubberies, was so eminently a residence; and she had never wanted to alter it into anything else, for it was so that she had found it when, on her mother-in-law's death, she and the young husband of so many years ago had first gone there to live. Rhoda must see her, her hair so smooth under its cap of snowy net, her black gowns—stuff for morning wear, silk for evening—so invariable, with the frills at neck and wrists, thick gold chains and the dim old brooches that went with them, as belonging almost to an epoch of albums on centre-tables, of Mendelssohn's sacred songs, and archery tournaments; an epoch of morning family-prayers and moral categories, where some people still believed in hell and everybody believed in sin. She didn't think that Rhoda had ever seen through all these alienating appearances to the reality she herself knew to be so different; but it had always been evident that she felt it through them; that she was at ease with her aunt, candid, even if angry, and willing, even when most silent and recalcitrant, to come down to Fernleigh, when her distracted parents could deal with her no longer, and to "think things over," as they put it to her, imploringly.

Mrs. Delafield could see Rhoda thinking things over from a very early age, from the earliest age at which recalcitrancy could count as practically alarming. She could see her walking slowly past this very border at the time that she had determined to go on the stage,—she had only just left the hands of her devastated governesses,—pausing now and then to examine unseeingly a plant, her hands clasped behind her, her dark, gloomy, lovely, young head brooding on the sense of wrong, and, even more, no doubt, on plots and stratagems. Her aunt had always watched her, while seeming, in the most comfortable manner possible, to give her no attention; noting everything about her,—and everything counted against poor Tim's and Frances's peace of mind,—from the slender, silken ankles to the tall column of the proud young throat; all of it, every bit of Rhoda, so determined by an insatiable vanity, which was the worst of her, and by a sardonic pride, which was the best.

Rhoda, to do her further justice, was even more wonderful in the eyes of her admirers than in her own. Her consciousness was not occupied so much with her own significance as with all the things due to it; and it was upon these things, and the methods of obtaining them, that she brooded as she walked. "Naughty girl," had been her aunt's unexpressed comment; and perhaps one reason why Rhoda had found it comfortable, or, at least, composing, to be with her, was that it was a relief to be seen as a naughty girl rather than as a terrifying portent.

Mrs. Delafield had determined at once that Rhoda should not go on the stage, though not, really, because Tim and Frances had begged her to dissuade the child. She could perfectly imagine having wished to go on the stage herself in her young days; and it was this consciousness, perhaps, that made her so fair to Rhoda's desire. She had taken her stand on no conventional objection; she had not even argued with Rhoda; she had simply been able to make her feel, bit by bit, that she hadn't one little atom of talent.

It had been the same thing, really, when Rhoda had announced her intention of marrying a dreadful young man, a bad young man,—Mrs. Delafield knew where to apply her categories,—who had a large studio where he gave teas and painted small, disagreeable pictures. They were clever pictures; Mrs. Delafield was aware of this, though Tim and Frances saw them only as disagreeable; and the young man, if bad, was clever. Mrs. Delafield had travelled up to town several times in this emergency, and had even accompanied Rhoda to the studio, where a young lady with bare legs and feet was dancing, with more concentration than spontaneity, before a cigaretted audience. Oddly enough, after this visit, it had been much easier to make Rhoda give up Mr. Austin Dell than it had been to make her give up the stage. Mrs. Delafield had merely talked him over, very mildly, him and his friends, asking here and there a kindly question about one or a slightly perplexed question about another. It had been Rhoda herself who had expressed awareness of the second-rate flavour that had brooded so heavily over dancer and audience, not leaving Mr. Dell himself untouched. On the point of Mr. Dell's income Mrs. Delafield soon felt that Rhoda knew misgivings—misgivings as to her own fitness to be a needy artist's wife. She made no overt recantation, but over her tea, presently, agreed with her aunt that it was a pity to dance with bare feet unless the feet were flawlessly well-shaped. "She is such a little fool, that Miss Matthews!" Rhoda had remarked. And after this there was no more talk of Mr. Dell.

II

WHEN, in the second year of the war, poor Tim and Frances, dusty, jaded, nearly shattered, but appeased at last, were able to announce the engagement of their daughter Rhoda to the unexceptionable Niel Quentyn, Mrs. Delafield's special function seemed ended; but, looking back over her long intercourse with her niece, she knew that Rhoda had felt her a relief rather than an influence; that she had made things easier rather than more difficult to her; that, in short, she had always successfully appealed to the girl's intelligence rather than to what poor Tim and Frances called her better self; and it was of Rhoda's intelligence, and of what possible pressure she might be able to bring to bear upon it, that she thought finally, as she worked at her border and waited for the fly that was to bring Rhoda's baby and its nurse from the station.

She had not been able to rejoice with her brother and his wife over Rhoda's match. She who had measured, during her years of acquaintanceship with her, her niece's force, had measured accurately, in her first glance at him, Niel's insignificance. He was good-looking, good-tempered, and very much in love; but caste, clothes, code, and the emotion of his age and situation summed him up. He had money, too, and could give Rhoda, together with a little handle to her name, the dim, rich, startling drawing-room in which her taste at once expressed itself, and a pleasant country house, where, as he confided to Mrs. Delafield, he hoped to inspire her, when the war was over, with his own ardour for hunting.

Rhoda was far too clever to quarrel with such excellent bread and butter; but what could he give her more? for Rhoda would want more than bread and butter; what food for excitement and adventure could he offer her indolent yet eager mind and her nature, at once so greedy and so fastidious? Mrs. Delafield asked herself the question, even while she watched Rhoda's wonderful white form move up the nave at her splendid, martial wedding; even while poor Frances wept for joy and "The Voice that breathed o'er Eden" surged from the organ; and she feared that Niel was getting far more than he had bargained for and Rhoda far less.

The first year, it was true, passed successfully. Poor Frances, who had, fortunately, died at the end of it, had known no reason for abated rejoicing. She lived long enough to see the baby, little Jane Amoret, as Rhoda persisted in calling the child; and she had welcomed Niel home once on leave—Niel as much infatuated as ever and trying to take an intelligent interest in Picasso. It was since then, during the past year, that Tim's letters had expressed a growing presage and appeal. Moved by the latter, and only a short time before her own grief had overtaken her, she had gone up to London and stayed with him for a few days, and had taken tea with Rhoda.

At Rhoda's it had been exactly as she expected. The drawing-room was worthy of its fame; so worthy that Mrs. Delafield wondered how Niel afforded it—and in war-time, too. Rhoda, as she often announced, was clever at picking up things, and many of the objects with which she had surrounded herself were undoubted trophies of her resource and knowledge. But all the taste and skill in the world didn't give one that air of pervading splendour, as of the setting for a Russian ballet, in which the red lacquer and the Chinese screens, the blacks and golds and rich, dim whites were, like Rhoda herself, sunken with her customary air of gloomy mirth in the deepest cushions and surpassingly dressed, merged in the soft, unstressed, yet magnificent atmosphere. It was the practical side of matters—the depth of good, dull Niel's purse measured against the depth of Rhoda's atmosphere—that alarmed Mrs. Delafield, rather than Rhoda herself and Rhoda's friends, of whom poor Tim had so distressingly written.

There were many suave and merry young men, mainly in khaki, and various ladies, acute or languorous, who had the air of being as carefully selected as the chairs and china. There were tea and cigarettes, and an abundance of wonderful talk that showed no sign of mitigation on account of her mid-Victorian presence; though, as Mrs. Delafield reflected, musing on the young people about her, no one could say, except their clever selves, how much mitigation there might not be. Like Rhoda, no doubt, they felt her reality through her mid-Victorianism. Her small black bonnet with its velvet strings, and her long, loose jacket trimmed with fringe, would not restrain them beyond a certain point. Yet she suspected that they had a point, and she wondered, though the question did not alarm her, where it could be placed.

They talked, at all events, and she listened; at times she even smiled; and since by no possibility could her smiles be taken as complicities, she was willing that they should be taken as comprehensions. Rhoda's friends, though so young, were chill and arid, and the enthusiasms they allowed themselves had the ring of provocation rather than of ardour. Yet she did not dislike them; they were none of them like Mr. Dell; and, though so withered by sophistication, they had at moments flashes of an uncanny, almost an ingenuous wisdom.

The occasion had not alarmed her, and she had found but one moment oppressive, that of the appearance—the displayal, as of a Chinese idol, indeed, or a Pekinese spaniel (Rhoda had three of these)—of poor little Jane Amoret. She rarely disliked her niece, even when feeling her most naughty;

but she found herself disliking her calculated maternity, with its kisses, embraces and reiterated "darlings." Jane Amoret had eyed her gravely and, as gravely, had held out her arms to her nurse to be taken back when the spectacle was over. Jane Amoret's attire was quite as strange as her mother's drawing-room, and Rhoda had contrived to make her look like a cross between an Aubrey Beardsley and a gorgeous, dressed-up doll Madonna in a Spanish cathedral.

On returning to Tim, Mrs. Delafield found that she could not completely reassure him, but she laid stress, knowing it would be, comparatively, a comfort, on Rhoda's extravagance, eliciting from him a groan of "I know!—I know!—Poor Niel's been writing to me about it!—Dances; dinners; gowns. One would say she had no conscience at all—and at a time like this!" But he went on, "That's nothing, though. That can be managed when Niel gets back—if he ever does, poor fellow!—and can put his foot down on the spot. You didn't see him, then? He wasn't there—the young man?"

Tim had never before spoken definitely of a young man.

"The young man?" she questioned. "There were a dozen of them. Of course, she'll have a special one: that's part of the convention. Rhoda may cultivate—like all the rest of them—every appearance of lawless attachment; but you may be sure, dear Tim, that it's only a pose, a formula, like the painted lips and dyed hair, which doesn't in the least mean they are demi-mondaines."

"Painted lips? Dyed hair? Demi-mondaines?" Tim had wanly echoed. "Do you really mean, Isabel, that Rhoda paints and dyes?"

"Not her hair. It's too lovely to be dyed. But her lips,—why, haven't you seen it?—ever since she was eighteen. It is all, as I say, a pose; a formula. They are all afraid of nothing so much as of seeming respectable. I imagine that there's just as much marital virtue at large in the world nowadays as when we were young.—Who is the young man?" she had, nevertheless, ended.

"My dear, don't ask me!" Tim had moaned, blanched and battered in his invalid's chair. (Why wouldn't he come down and live with her? Why, indeed, except that, since Frances's death, he had felt that he must stand by, in London, and watch over Rhoda.) "I only know what I've heard. Amy has talked and talked. And everybody else is talking, according to her." Amy was Frances's sister, a well-meaning, but disturbing woman, with a large family of well-conducted, well-married, unpainted, and unfashionable daughters. "She is here every day about it. They are always together. He is always there. The poet—the new young poet. He has a heart or a chest or a stomach—

something that has sent him home and that keeps him safe at Whitehall, while poor Niel fights in France. Surely, Isabel, you've heard of Christopher Darley? Wasn't he there? Young. Younger than Rhoda. Black hair. Big eyes. Silent."

Silent.—Yes, there had been, beside Jane Amoret, one silent person in Rhoda's drawing-room. And she had been aware of him constantly, though, till now, unconsciously. Very young; very pale; aloof, near a window, with an uncalculated aloofness. She reconstructed an impression that became deeper the further she went into it. Thick backward locks that had given his forehead a wind-blown look, and a gaze now and then directed on herself, a gaze grave, withdrawing, yet scrutinizing, too.

"Yes; I think, now that you describe him, I must have seen him," she murmured; while a curious alarm mounted in her, an alarm that none of Rhoda's more characteristic circle had aroused. "He wasn't living by a formula of freedom," she reflected. "And he wasn't arid." Aloud she said, "He looked a nice young creature, I remember."

"He writes horrible poems, Amy says; blasphemous. There they are. I can't understand them. He casts down everything; has no beliefs of any kind. Nice? I should think that's the last adjective that would describe him."

She had picked up the unobtrusive volume and found herself arrested; not as she had been by the memory of the young man's gaze, nor yet in the manner that Tim's account indicated; but still arrested. Very young—but austere, dignified, and strange, genuinely and effortlessly strange. So a young priest might have written, seeking in close-pressed metaphysical analogies to find expression for spiritual passion. She stood, puzzled and absorbed.

"No, it isn't blasphemous," she said presently. "And he has beliefs. But surely, Tim dear, surely this young man can't care for Rhoda."

How could a young man who wrote like that about the mystic vision care for Rhoda?

"Not care for Rhoda!" Tim's voice had now the quaintest ring of paternal resentment. "The most beautiful young woman in London! Why, he's head over heels in love with her. And the worst of it is that, from what Amy sees and hears, she cares for him."

"It's curious," Mrs. Delafield said, laying down the book. "I shouldn't have thought he'd care about beautiful young women."

And now Tim's letter, on this December morning, announced that Rhoda had gone off with Christopher Darley; and Mrs. Delafield could find it in her heart, as she worked and pondered, to wish that her dear Tim had followed Frances before this catastrophe overtook him.

"Good heavens!" she heard herself muttering, "if only she'd been meaner, more cowardly, and stayed and lied—as women of her kind are supposed to do. If only she'd let him die in peace; he can't have many years."

But no: it had been done with le beau geste. Tim had known nothing, and poor Niel, home for his first peace leave, had come to him, bewildered and aghast, with the news. He had found a letter waiting for him, sent from the country. Tim copied the letter for her:—

DEAR NIEL:

I'm sure you felt, too, that our life couldn't go on. It had become too unsatisfactory for both of us. Luckily we are sensible people nowadays, and such mistakes can be remedied. You must mend your life as I am mending mine. I am leaving you, with Christopher Darley. I am so sorry if it seems sudden; but I felt it better that we should not meet again.

Yours affectionately

RHODA

"If only the poet hadn't had money, too!" Mrs. Delafield had thought. For this fact she had learned about Mr. Darley in London. Rhoda would never have abandoned that drawing-room had she not been secure of another as good.

Tim wrote that nothing could have been manlier, more generous, than Niel's behaviour. He was willing, for the sake of the child, to take Rhoda back, reinstate her, and protect her from the consequences of her act; and what Tim now begged of his sister was that she should see Rhoda, see if, confronting her, she could not induce her to return to her husband. Meanwhile Jane Amoret would be dispatched at once with her nurse to Fernleigh. Tim had written to his child in her retreat, and had implored her to go to her aunt. "I told her that you would receive her, Isabel," so Tim's letter ended; "and I trust you now to save us—as far as we can be saved. Tell her that her husband will forgive, and that I forgive, if she will return. Let her see the child. Let that be your appeal."

Poor, darling Tim! Very mid-Victorian. "Forgive." Would "receive" her. The words had an antediluvian ring. With what battledore and shuttle-cock of mirth and repartee they would be sent sailing and spinning in Rhoda's world. All the same, she, who was mid-Victorian in seeming rather than in reality, would make other appeals, if Rhoda came. Already she could almost count the steady heads of her intentions thrusting up as if through the ground. Even in Rhoda's world repartee and mirth might be displayed rather than acted upon, and Rhoda might find herself, as a result of le beau geste, less favourably placed for the creation of another drawing-room than she imagined. That, of course, was the line to take with Rhoda; and as she reflected, carefully now, on what she would say to her,—as she determined that Rhoda should not leave her until she had turned her face firmly homeward,—the sound of wheels came up the road, and outside the high walls she heard the station fly drawing up at her gates. In another moment she was welcoming Jane Amoret and her nurse.

III

SHE had not seen the child for five months now, and her first glance at her, for all its sweetness, brought something of a shock, revealing as it did how deeply she cared for the little creature. She was not a child-lover, not undiscriminatingly fond of all examples of the undeveloped, though her kind solicitude might have given her that appearance. Children had always affected her, from the cradle, as personalities; and some, like the mature, were lovable and some the reverse. Jane Amoret had already paid her more than one visit—she had been more than willing that Rhoda should find her a convenience in this respect; and she had, from the first, found her lovable. But the five months had brought much more to the mere charm of babyhood. She was now potent and arresting in her appeal and dignity. She sat in her nurse's arms, her eyes fixed on her great-aunt, and, as Mrs. Delafield held out her hands to her, she unhesitatingly, if unsmilingly, answered, leaning forward to be taken.

She was a pale, delicate baby, her narrow little face framed in straightly cut dark hair, her mournful little lips only tinted with a rosy mauve; and, under long, fine brows, her great eyes were full of meditativeness. Rhoda, though now so richly a brunette, had, as a baby, been ruddy-haired and rosy-cheeked, with eyes of a velvety, submerging darkness. Jane Amoret's grey iris rayed out from the expanded pupil like the corolla of a flower. There was no likeness between the child and her mother. Nor was there anything of Niel's sleepy young countenance, with its air of still waters running shallow.

Mrs. Delafield, something of a student of heredity, saw in the little face an almost uncanny modern replica of her own paternal grandmother, whose pensive gaze, under high-dressed powdered hair, had followed her down the drawing-room in the home of her childhood. In Jane Amoret she recovered the sense of that forgotten romance of her youth—the wonderful, beautiful great-grandmother with the following eyes. Had they not, even then, been asking something of her?

"It isn't everyone she'll go to, ma'am," said the nurse, as they went up the path to the house, Mrs. Delafield carrying Jane Amoret.

Nurse was a highly efficient example of her type—crisp, cheerful, a little glib. Mrs. Delafield had never warmly liked her, and felt convinced now, that in spite of her decorous veneer of reticence, the servants' hall would be enlightened as to the whole story before many hours were over. Well, it could not be helped.

They went up to the big nursery overlooking the walled garden at the back of the house, where, since the morning's post and its announcements, a great fire of logs had been blazing. Nurse made but one respectful, passing reference to Rhoda. The country air would do Lady Quentyn good. She had, nurse thought, over-tired herself of late. What else she thought, Parton and the others were soon to hear hinted. And as Rhoda's calculated maternity had chilled her aunt on that day five months ago, so she was chilled now to think that Rhoda should have had more taste in the choice of her drawing-room than in that of her baby's nurse.

While, in the next room, the unpleasing woman was unpacking her own and Jane Amoret's effects, Mrs. Delafield was left alone with the child. She had found, on a shelf, a box of well-worn blocks, and seating herself in the low, chintz-covered wicker chair beside the fire, she placed them, one by one, before Jane Amoret, who, on her white wool rug, gave them a gentle attention. She had been too young for blocks on her last visit.

The old chair, as Mrs. Delafield moved in it, leaning down, creaked softly, and she remembered, a curious excitement stirring under all these recoveries of the past, that it had been condemned as really too decrepit when Peggy had been a baby. Yet the threat had never been carried out. It had gone on through Peggy's babyhood and through the babyhood of Peggy's children, and, unused for all these years, here it gave forth again just the plaintive yet comfortable sounds which, even more, it seemed, than another baby's presence, evoked Peggy and her own young maternity.

The chair, the blocks, the firelight playing on the happy walls, with their framed Caldecotts and Cherry Ripes and Bubbles, all evoked that past, filling her with the mingled acquiescence and yearning of old age. And Jane Amoret evoked a past far, far more distant. Peggy had not been like the great-grandmother. None of them had ever reincarnated that vanished loveliness. But here, mysterious and appealing, it was before her; and it seemed to brush across her very heartstrings every time that, from the blocks, the child lifted the meditative grey of her eyes to her great-aunt's face.

Far too mysterious, far too lovely, far too gentle, this frail potentiality, for any uses ever to be made of it by Rhoda, by Niel, or by nurse. And the yearning became a yearning over Jane Amoret.

Yes, there the edifice rose, block by block—her deft, deliberate fingers placed them one after the other, under Jane Amoret's eyes, absorbed in this towering achievement. The miniature Alhambra finished, she sat and gazed, and her little chest lifted in a great sigh of wonder and appeasement. Then, her baby interest dropping, she looked round at the flames, and, for a little time, gazed at them, while her great-aunt's hand moved softly to rest upon her head. It seemed then, as if in answer to the rapt and tender look bent above her, that Jane Amoret's eyes were again raised and that she stretched up her arms to be taken.

"She really loves me," said Mrs. Delafield, as touched and trembling as a young lover. She lifted her, pressing the little body against her breast; and, as Jane Amoret gave herself to the enfolding, a thought that was as sharp and as sudden as a pang flashed through her great-aunt's mind. "I can never give her up."

What came to her first, as she sat there, Jane Amoret's head leaning against her, was the thought of Christmas roses. It was a gift, a miracle. And to what depths of loneliness the gift had been given; with what depths of life she answered it! But she was breathless while she tried to think, knowing something terrible in her own swift acceptance; seeing for the first time something lawless and perilous in her own nature. Never in her life had she betrayed a trust; never broken a law. Yet often, through the years, she had paused, contemplative and questioning, to gaze at something her mirror showed her, an implication that only she could see, a capacity never realized. And what she saw sometimes, with discomfort and shrinking, in those freaked eyes, those firm lips, was an untamed wildness that had come to her from much further back than a great-grandmother; something predatory and reckless, perhaps from the days of border robbers, and Highland chiefs whose only law was their own will.

She knew now what were the faces waiting to seize upon her accusingly. Not Rhoda's. She swept Rhoda and her forfeited claim aside. Let her stay with her poet, since that was what she had chosen. It was Niel and poor Tim who looked at her aghast. But another face hovered softly and effacingly before them; a pale young face with rosy-mauve lips and following eyes that said, "They will never understand me. This is what I was trying to tell you, always. I knew that I was coming back. This is what I was asking you to do."

It was superstition; it did not deceive her for a moment. Desire dressing itself in a supernatural appeal. Absurd and discreditable. But, in all truth and honour, wasn't there something in it? Wasn't there a time, once in a blue moon, for lawlessness, when it came as a miracle? Whom would she harm, really? What could his paternity mean, really, to drowsy young Niel? And could she not salve Tim's wounds?

The only thing that could count,—she came to that at last, feeling the child, with sleeping, drooping head and little hands held within her hand, already so profoundly her own,—the only thing was Jane Amoret herself. Had she a right to keep her from what was, perhaps, her chance of the normal, even if the defective, life? Wasn't even a bad and foolish mother better than no mother at all, and an untarnished name supremely desirable? She struggled, her eyes fixed on the fire, her hand unconsciously closing fast on the little intertwined hands within it. And with the face of the great-grandmother came again the thought of the Christmas roses, of the gift, the miracle.

She had not sought anything. She had not even chosen. It was rather as if Jane Amoret had chosen her. She need not make an effort to keep the gift. She need merely make no effort to give it back. If Rhoda came (oh, she could but pray that Rhoda would not come!), she need not find the right words for her. She had only to remain the passive spectator of Rhoda's enterprise and not put out a hand to withdraw her from it. And, thrusting, feverishly, final decisions from her, her mind sprang out into far projects and promises. She could, with a will, live for twenty more years yet and fill them full for Jane Amoret. Niel must not lose his child, evidently. She would arrange with Niel. He had always liked her and turned to her. Let this be his home, and welcome. But of course, he would marry again. She could persuade him not to take Jane Amoret from her to give to a step-mother. Niel would be easy.

And Tim, now, must come, of course. Tim should, with her, enjoy Jane Amoret to the full. What a happy childhood she could make it! It was, to begin with, quite the happiest nursery she knew, this long-empty nursery of hers. In a few years' time Jane Amoret would be old enough to have her own little plot in the garden—Peggy's plot; and a pony like Peggy's should come to the empty stables. She saw already the merry, instructed girl she would choose as Jane Amoret's governess: some one young enough to play out of lesson hours; some one who would teach her to know birds and flowers as well as history and Latin. She would keep Jane Amoret's hair cut like this,—it was the only point in the child's array in which her taste was Rhoda's,—straight across the forehead and straight across the neck, until she was fifteen, and she should wear smocked blue linen for morning and white for afternoon, as her own children had done. With good luck, she might even see Jane Amoret married.

Actually, she was thinking about Jane Amoret's marriage, actually wondering about the nice little eldest boy at the manor,—while her arms tightened in instinctive maternal anxiety around the sleeping baby,—when Parton, doing her best not to look round-eyed, announced Lady Quentyn.

IV

SHE knew, as she waited for Rhoda to come up, that something she had forgotten during this last half-hour—perhaps it was her conscience—steeled her suddenly to the endurance of a test. Tim had worded it, "Let her see the child. Let that be your appeal." Would it not appease her conscience to stand or fall by that? It should be her appeal. But the only one.

Jane Amoret had waked, and now, dazed but unfretful, suffered herself to be placed again on the rug among the blocks, one of which Mrs. Delafield put into her hands, bidding her build a beautiful big house, as great-aunt had done. The anguish of her own suspense was made manifest to her in the restless gesture with which, after that, and while she waited, she bent to put another log on the fire.

Rhoda's soft, deliberate rustle was outside. In another moment she had entered, and the effect that Mrs. Delafield dreaded seemed produced on the spot; for, arrested at the very threshold, almost before her eyes had sought her aunt's, Rhoda stared down at the child with knotted, with even incredulous brows.

"Oh! He's sent her already, then!" she exclaimed.

What did the stare, the exclamation, portend?

"Yes. He sent her, of course, as soon as he came back."

"But why?—until our interview is over?"

"Why not? She'd been alone for a week." Mrs. Delafield spoke with the mildness which, she determined, should not leave her. "Niel, of course, wanted to have her cared for."

Rhoda, during this little interchange, had remained near the door; but now, perceiving, perhaps, that she had come near to giving herself away, she cleared her brows of their perplexity and moved forward to the fire, where, leaning her velvet elbow on the mantelpiece, she answered, drily laughing; "Oh! Niel's care! He wouldn't know whether the child were fed on suet-pudding or cold ham! She's not alone, with nurse. There's no one who can take such care of her as nurse. I knew that." And she went on immediately, putting the question of Jane Amoret's presence behind her with decision, "Well, poor Aunt Isabel, what have you to say to me? Father wrote that you would consent to be the go-between. He absolutely implored me to come, and it's to satisfy him I'm here, for I really can't imagine what good it can do."

No; Mrs. Delafield had grasped her own security and her own danger. It had not been in remorse or tenderness that Rhoda's eyes had fixed themselves upon her child, it had been in anxiety, lest Jane Amoret's presence should be the signal of some final verdict against her. She had come because she hoped to be taken back; and if there was all the needed justification in Rhoda's callousness, there was an undreamed-of danger in her expectation.

"Well, we must see," Mrs. Delafield remarked; and already she was measuring the necessities of Rhoda's pride against the urgencies of Rhoda's disenchantment. It was Rhoda's pride that she must hold to. Rhoda, even if she had come, had only come to make her own terms.

"Did you motor over?" she asked. "You are not very far from here, are you?"

No train could have brought her at that hour.

"Twenty miles or so away," said Rhoda. "I was able to hire a motor, a horrible, open affair with torn flaps that let in all the air, so that I'm frozen."

Her loveliness did, indeed, look a little pinched and sharpened, and there was more than the cold drive to account for it. But she was still surpassingly lovely, with the loveliness that, once you were confronted with it, seemed to explain everything that might need explanation. That was Rhoda's strongest card. She left her appearance to speak for her and made no explanations, as now, when, indeed, she had all the air of expecting other people to make them. But her aunt only said, while Jane Amoret, from her rug, kept her grave gaze upon her mother, "Won't you have some hot milk?"

"Thanks, yes, I should be glad of it," said Rhoda. "How lucky you are to have it. We are given only condensed for our coffee at the hotel. It's quite revolting." And after Mrs. Delafield had rung, and since no initiative came from her, she was, in a manner, forced to open the conversation. "Niel has only himself to thank," she said. "He's been making himself too impossible for a long time."

"Really? In what way? Perhaps the hard life over there has affected his temper."

Mrs. Delafield allowed herself the irony. Rhoda, indeed, must expect that special flavour from her.

"Something has certainly affected it," said Rhoda, drawing a chair to the fire and spreading her beautiful hands before it. "I'm quite tired, I confess,—horrid as I'm perfectly aware it sounds to say it,—of hearing about the hard life. Life's hard enough for all of us just now, heaven knows; and I think they haven't had half a bad time over there, numbers of them—men like Niel, I mean, who've travelled comfortably about the world and never had the least little wound, nor been, ever, in any real danger, as far as I can make out; at least, not since he's had the staff work. It's very different from my poor Christopher, who rotted in the cold and mud until it nearly killed him. There would be some point in his talking of a hard life."

This was all very illuminating, and the bold advance of Christopher won Mrs. Delafield's admiration for its manner; but she passed it over to inquire again, "In what way has Niel been making himself impossible?" The more impossible Rhoda depicted him, the easier to leave her there, shut out by his impossibility.

"Why, his meanness," said Rhoda, her cold, dark eyes, as she turned them upon her aunt, expressing, indeed, quite a righteous depth of reprobation. "For months and months it's been the same wearisome cry. He's written about nothing but economy, fussing, fuming, and preaching. It's so ugly, at his time of life."

"Have you been a little extravagant, perhaps? Everything is so much more costly, isn't it? He may well have been anxious about your future, and the child's."

It was perfectly mild, and the irony Rhoda would expect from her.

"Oh, no he wasn't," said Rhoda, now with her gloomy laugh. "He was anxious about his hunting. I don't happen to care for that primitive form of amusement, and Niel doesn't happen to care about anything else; certainly he doesn't care about beauty, and that's all I do care about. So in his view, since, precisely, life has become so costly, beauty had to go to the wall and I mustn't dress decently or have a decently ordered house. I haven't been in the least extravagant," said Rhoda. "I've known what it is to be cold; I've known what it is to be hungry; it's been, at times, literally impossible to get food and coal in London. Oh, you don't know anything about it, Aunt Isabel, tucked away comfortably down here with logs and milk. And if Niel had had any appreciation of the position and had realized at all that I prefer being hungry to being ill-dressed, he would have turned his mind to cutting down his own extravagances and offered to allow me"—and now, for an instant, if velvet can show sharpness, Mrs. Delafield caught in the sliding velvet eye an evident edge of cogitation, even, of calculation—"at least two thousand a year for myself. Money buys absolutely nothing nowadays."

So there it was, and it amounted to an offer. Or, rather, it amounted to saying that it was the sum for which she would be willing to consider any offer of Niel's. Mrs. Delafield, measuring still Rhoda's pride against Rhoda's urgency, mused on her velvet garments, the fur that broadly bordered her skirts, slipped from her shoulders, and framed her hands. Poor Tim had been able to give his daughter only a few hundred a year, and Niel's hunting must indeed have been in danger. Rhoda's pride, she knew, stood, as yet, between herself and any pressure from the urgency; she could safely leave the offer to lie and go on presently to question, "And you'll be better off now?"

Inevitably unsuspecting as she was, Rhoda, all the same, must feel an unexpectedness in her attitude, and at this it was with a full, frank sombreness that she turned her gaze upon her. Anything but a fool she had always been, and she answered, after the moment of gloomy scrutiny, "Don't imagine, please, Aunt Isabel, that because I speak openly of practical matters I left Niel to get a better establishment. I left him because I didn't love him. I was willing to sacrifice anything rather than stay. Because it is a sacrifice. I took the step I've taken under no illusion. We are too uncivilized yet for things to be anything but difficult for a woman who takes the step, and the brave people have to pay for the cowards and hypocrites."

This, somehow, was not at all Rhoda's own note. Mrs. Delafield felt sure she caught an echo of Mr. Darley's ministrations. She was glad that Rhoda should receive them: they would sustain her; and since she was determined—or almost—that Rhoda should stay with Mr. Darley, it was well that she should receive all the sustainment possible.

"It certainly must require great love and great courage," she assented.

Rhoda's eyes still sombrely scrutinized her. "I didn't expect you to see it, I confess, Aunt, Isabel."

"Oh, but I do," said Mrs. Delafield.

The milk was now brought and Rhoda began to sip it.

"As for my being better off, since you are kind enough to take an interest in that aspect of my situation," she went back, "Christopher hasn't, it's true, as much money as Niel. But our tastes are the same, so that I shall certainly be very much better off. We shall live in London—after Niel sets me free." And here again she just glanced at her aunt, who bowed assent, murmuring, "Yes; yes; he is quite willing to set you free; at once."—"And until then," Rhoda went on, as if she hadn't needed the assurance,—second-rate assurance as, Mrs. Delafield felt sure, she found it,—"and until then I shall stay in the country. Christopher has his post still at the Censor's office, and won't, I'm afraid, get his demobilization for some time. He translates things, you know. So we are going to find a little old house, for me,—we are looking for one now,—and I shall see a few friends there, quite quietly, and Christopher can come up and down, until everything is settled. I think that's the best plan."

Rhoda spoke with a dignity that had even a savour of conscious sweetness, and, as Mrs. Delafield reflected, was running herself very completely into her corner.

There was silence now for a little while. Rhoda finished her milk, and Jane Amoret, gently and unobtrusively moving among her blocks, succeeded, at length, in balancing the last one on her edifice and looked up at her great-aunt for approbation.

"Very good, darling. A beautiful house," said Mrs. Delafield, leaning over her, but with a guarded tenderness. What a serpent she had become! There was Rhoda's jealousy to look out for. She might imagine herself fond of Jane Amoret, if she saw that some one else adored her.

"She's quite used to you already, isn't she?" said Rhoda, watching them. "I wonder what you'll make of her. She strikes me as rather a dull little thing, though she's certainly very pretty. She's rather like Niel, isn't she? Though she certainly isn't as dull as Niel!" She laughed slightly. "All the same,"—and Mrs. Delafield now, in Rhoda's voice, scented the close approach of danger, and was aware, though she did not look up to meet it, that Rhoda's eyes took on a new watchfulness,—"All the same I must consider the poor little thing's future. That is, of course, my one real difficulty."

"Was it? In going away? In having left her, you mean?" Mrs Delafield prayed that her mildness might gloss, to Rhoda's ear, the transition to conscious combat that her instinctive change of tense revealed to her own. "Oh, but you need not do that. Don't let that trouble you for a moment, Rhoda. I will take charge of her—complete charge. I can do it easily. My house is empty, and the child will be a companion to me. I don't find her dull. She is a dear little thing, so good and gentle. You need really have no anxiety."

"Oh, I see." Rhoda was gazing at her earnestly. "Thanks. That's certainly a relief. Though all the same I don't suppose you'd claim that you could replace the child's mother."

"Yes. I think so, Rhoda. A mother who had left her for a lover."

Mrs. Delafield kept her eyes fixed on the fire. Rhoda stood up and leaned her back against the mantelpiece. She could no longer control the manifestations of her impatience and her perplexity.

"That would be your view, of course; and father's; and Niel's. It's not mine. I consider the responsibility to be Niel's." "Well, whosesoever the responsibility, the deed is done, isn't it?" Mrs. Delafield observed. "I'm not arraigning you, you know. I'm merely stating the fact. You have left her."

Rhoda's impatience now visibly brushed past these definitions. "You say that Niel is ready to set me free. I took that for granted, of course. It's only common decency. But that's hardly what father could have meant in imploring me to come to—you. He told me nothing—only implored, and lamented. And, since I am here, I'd like some information, I confess."

It was the first step away from pride, and it was a long one. And Mrs. Delafield knew that with it came her own final turning-point. Here, at this moment, she must be true to Tim and Niel, or betray their trust. And here no less—for so it seemed to her—she might, in betraying them, take the law into her own hands and promise herself, and them, that, in breaking it, she would make something better. Yet she did not feel these alternatives, now, at war within her mind. She knew that they were there, implicit, but she knew them already answered. Rhoda had answered for her; and Jane Amoret had answered. It took her, however, a moment to find her own answer, the verbal one, and while she looked for it, she kept her eyes on the fire.

"Your father wants you to go back," she said at last. "Niel is willing to take you back. That is the information I had for you. Not for a moment because he would accept your interpretation of responsibility, and not for a moment because of any personal feeling for you; which must be a relief to you. Merely for your sake, and the child's. But I don't know how to plead such a cause with you, Rhoda. I understand you, I think, better than your father does. I've always seen your point of view as he could never see it, and I see it even now. So that I should feel that I asked you something outrageous in asking you to go back to your husband when you love another man. If you should want to go back, that would be a very different matter—if, by chance, you feel you've made a mistake and are tired, already, of Mr. Darley."

She had time, in the pause that followed, the scales pulsing almost evenly—it was as if she saw them—between Rhoda's pride and Rhoda's urgency, to wonder at herself. And most of all to wonder that she regretted nothing. She kept her eyes on the fire, but she knew that Rhoda, very still, scrutinized her intently. The sharply drawn tension of the moment had resolved itself, to her imagination, into a series of tiny ticks, as if of the scales settling down to the choice, before Rhoda spoke. Then what she found to say was, "That's hardly likely, is it?"

"I felt it impossible, you will be glad to hear," said Mrs. Delafield. "No one who understands you could suspect you, whatever your faults, of two infidelities in the space of a fortnight."

And now again there was a long silence, broken only by the lapping of the flames up the chimney and the soft movements of Jane Amoret among her blocks.

Rhoda turned away at last, facing the fire and looking down at it, her hands on the edge of the mantelpiece, her foot on the fender; and she presently lifted the foot and dealt the logs a kick.

It was all clear to Mrs. Delafield. She was tired of her poet, or, at all events, did not, in the new life, find compensations enough. She had come, hoping to have her way made clear for a reëntry, dignified, if not triumphant, into the old life. And here she was, in her corner, her head fairly fixed to the wall.

Meanwhile, what had become of the mid-Victorian conscience? What had, indeed, become of any conscience at all, since she continued to regret nothing? She even found excuses, perfidious, no doubt, yet satisfactory. It had been the truth she had given Rhoda—the real truth, her own, if not the truth she owed her, not the truth as Tim and Niel had placed it, all confidently, in her hands. But since it was preëminently not the truth that Rhoda had come to seize, she was willing, now that she had fixed her so firmly, to give her something else, and she really rejoiced to find it ready, going on presently and with a note of relief that Rhoda's ear could not fail to catch:—

"Not only from the point of view of dignity one couldn't suspect it of you, Rhoda, but—I want to say it to you, having had my glimpse of Mr. Darley—from the point of view of taste. If you were going to do anything of this sort,—and I don't need to tell you how deeply I deplore it nor how wrong I think you,—but if you were going to do it, you couldn't have chosen better. He is gifted; he is charming; he is good. I saw it all at once."

There was her further truth, and really it was due to Rhoda. Rhoda, at this, faced her again and, highly civilized creature that she was, it was with her genuine grim mirth.

"Upon my word, Aunt Isabel!" she commented. "You are astonishing."

"Am I? Why?" asked Mrs. Delafield, though she knew quite well.

"Why, my dear? Because you are over sixty years old and you wear caps. I expected to find dismay, reproach, and lamentations—all the strains of poor old father's harmonium; to have you down on your knees begging me to return to the paths of virtue. And here you are, cool and unperturbed and, positively, patting us on the back; positively giving us your blessing. Well, well, wonders will never cease! Yes, he is charming, no one can deny that; and good and gifted, too. But to think of your having spotted it so quickly! Why, you only saw him once, if I remember, and I don't remember that you talked at all."

"We didn't. I only saw him once."

"And it was enough! To make you understand! To make you condone!—Come, out with it, Aunt Isabel, you wicked old lady! I see now why I've always got on so well with you. You are wicked."

"To make me understand. I won't say condone."

"You needn't say it. You've said enough. And certainly it is a feather in Christopher's cap. But he is the sort of person one falls in love with at first sight."

"So I see."

"And so do I," said Rhoda, still laughing. But her slightly avenging gaiety dropped from her after the last sally, and turning again to the fire, and again kicking her log, she said, almost sombrely, "He absolutely worships me."

Was not this everybody's justification? Mrs. Delafield seized it, rising, as on a satisfying close.

"Will you stay to lunch?" she asked.

"Dear me, no!" Rhoda laughed. "I must get back to Christopher. And the motor is there waiting. So you'll write to father and tell him that I came here and that you advised me to stick to Christopher."

"Advised? Have I seemed to advise, Rhoda? Do you mean"—it was, Mrs. Delafield knew, the final peril—"that you had considered not sticking to him?"

Rhoda continued to laugh a little, drawing up her furs.

"Rather not! It couldn't have entered my head, could it, either from the point of view of dignity or of taste—as you've been telling me? You have been very wonderful, you know! Tell father, then, if you like, that you gave us your blessing."

"I'll tell him," said Mrs. Delafield, "that I'm convinced you ought not to go back to Niel."

"I see,"—Rhoda nodded, and their eyes sounded each other, curiously,—"though father thinks I ought."

"Of course. That's why you're here."

"Father would have gone down on his knees to beg me."

"Yes. Down on his knees. Poor Tim!"

She was horribly frightened, but she faced Rhoda's grim mirth deliberate with gravity. And Rhoda, whatever she might have seen or guessed, accepted her defeat; accepted the dignity and taste thrust upon her. "Father, in other words, isn't a wicked old gentleman as you are a wicked old lady. I see it all, and it's all a feather in Christopher's cap. Well, Aunt Isabel, good-bye. Shall I see you again? Will you come and call when I'm Mrs. Darley? I don't see how, with a clear conscience, you can chuck us, you know."

"Nor do I," Mrs. Delafield conceded, after only a pause. "I don't often go to London, but, when I do, I shall look in upon you, if you want me to."

"Rather!" Rhoda, now gloved and muffled, had fallen back on her normal rich economy of speech. "You'll be useful as well as pleasant. And Christopher will adore you, I'm sure. I'll tell him that you think him charming."

"Do," said Mrs. Delafield, following her to the door.

She had forgotten even to kiss Jane Amoret good-bye.

V

Still Mrs. Delafield knew no remorse. Rather, a wine-like elation filled her. She thought of her state of consciousness in terms of wine, and ordered up from her modest cellar a special old port, hardly tasted since her husband's death, and, all alone, drank at lunch a little glass in honour of Jane Amoret's advent. Also, though elated, she was conscious of needing a stimulant. The scene with Rhoda had cost her more than could, at the moment, be quite computed.

What it had won for her she was able to compute when, after lunch, she went upstairs to look at Jane Amoret asleep in her white cot. She did not feel like a robber brooding in guilty joy over ill-gotten booty. She could not feel herself that, nor Jane Amoret booty. Jane Amoret was treasure, pure heaven-sent treasure, her flower of miracle. Christmas roses had been in her mind since morning, and the darkness, the whiteness of the child, as well as her beautiful unexpectedness, made her think of them anew; her gravity, too; something of melancholy that the flowers embodied; for they were not smiling flowers—gazing rather at the wintry sky in earnest meditation.

Jane Amoret's black lashes lay upon her cheek, ever so slightly turned up at the tips, and her great-aunt, leaning over her, felt herself doting upon them and upon the little softly breathing profile embedded in the pillow, a bud-like, folded hand beside it.

"Little darling, we will make each other happy," she whispered.

Rhoda had passed from their lives like a storm-cloud.

Jane Amoret was still sleeping, and she had gone downstairs to the little morning-room where, since the war, she had really lived, to settle with herself what she must say to Tim, when there came a ringing at the front-door bell. The morning-room, at the back of the house, like the nursery, overlooked the southern lawn and the walls of the kitchen-garden; but she could usually hear if a motor drove up, and, in her still concentration upon the empty sheet lying before her on the desk, she was aware that there had been no sound. It was too early for a visitor, too early for the post, and she looked up with some curiosity as Parton came in.

"It's a gentleman, ma'am, to see you," said Parton; and her young, trained visage showed signs of a discomfiture deeper than that Rhoda's coming had evoked. "Mr. Darley, ma'am; and he hopes very much you are disengaged."

Mrs. Delafield had, as a first sensation, that of sympathy with Parton. Parton evidently knew all about it and was evidently in distress lest her face betrayed her knowledge. In her effort to maintain her own standards of impassivity she suddenly blushed crimson, and Mrs. Delafield then felt that she was very old and Parton very young, and that in that fact alone was a bond, even if there had been no other. She had many bonds with Parton, and now, seeing her so soft, uncertain, and dismayed, she would have liked to pat her on the shoulder and say, "There, my dear, it doesn't make any difference. I assure you I'm not disturbed." And since she could not say it, she looked it, replying with the utmost equability, "Mr. Darley? By all means. Show him in at once, Parton."

There was, after Parton had gone, a short interval, while Mr. Darley doubtless was taking off his coat, and during which she felt herself mainly engaged in maintaining her equability. But, after her encounter with Rhoda, wasn't she equable enough for any situation? Besides, Mr. Darley could in no fashion menace Jane Amoret, and under all her conjectures and amazements there lay a certain satisfaction. She knew, from her encounter with Parton, that she was interested in all young creatures when they were nice, and she was not sorry to have another look at Mr. Darley.

When he entered and she saw him,—not in khaki as that first time, but in a gray tweed suit,—when Parton had softly and securely closed the door and left them together, she found herself borne along on a curious deepening of the current of sympathy for mere youth. She had not remembered how young he was; she had not had that as her dominant impression at Rhoda's tea, as she had it now. He must be several years younger than Rhoda; hardly more than twenty-two or three, she thought; and it must have been as a mere child that the war had swept him out into maturing initiations. Something of an experience, shattering yet solidifying, was in his face, fragile, wasted, yet more final and finished than one would have expected at his time of life; and also, in curious contrast to his boyish, beardless look, a deep line was engraved across his forehead; whether by suffering or by the trick she soon discovered in him of raising his eyebrows in an effort of intense concentration, she could not tell.

She gave him her hand simply, and said, "Do sit down."

But Mr. Darley, though he looked at the chair she indicated, did not take it. He remained standing on the hearthrug, facing the windows, his hands clasped behind him, and she then became aware that he was enduring a veritable agony of shyness. It did not take the form of blushes,—though his was a girlish skin that would display them instantly,—or of awkward gestures or faltering speech. It was a shyness wild, still, and bereft of all appeal, like that of a bird,—the simile came sharply to her,—a bird that had followed some swift impulse and that now, caught in a sudden hand, relapsed into utter immobility. His large eyes were on hers—fixed. His expression was like a throbbing heart. She knew that all she wanted, for the moment, was to show him that the hand was gentle.

"I'm afraid you came hoping to find Rhoda," she said, looking away from him and giving her chair, as a pretext, sundry little adjustments before drawing it to the fire. "But she left this morning, after seeing me, and you must have crossed her on the road. At least—have you motored?"

The large eyes, she found, were still fixed on her as, with the question, she glanced up at him; but he answered immediately—rather as if with a croaking cry from the blackbird when one pressed it,—

"No; I came by train. I left a little after Rhoda did."

"By train?" she marvelled kindly. "But we are four miles from the station here. Aren't you, at your end, as far? And such roads!" She saw now that his boots and upturned trousers were, indeed, deeply mired.

"Oh—I didn't mind the walk," said Mr. Darley. "It wasn't far."

She was sure he hadn't found it far. His whole demeanour expressed the overmastering impulse that had, till then, sustained him.

"Have you had any lunch?" she went on. "I can't think where you can have lunched. There's nothing at the station. Do let me send for something. I've only just finished."

It seemed strangely indicated that she should, to-day, feed Rhoda and her lover.

But the caught blackbird was in no state for feeding. More wildly, yet more faintly than before he gave forth the croaking cry with, "Oh, no. Thanks so much. Yes. At our station. I found something at our station. Sandwiches; no, a bun. I had a cup of Bovril."

And now, curiously, poignantly to her, he began to blush as though suddenly and overwhelmingly aware of himself and of how idiotically he must be behaving. Poor child! How young he was! And how ill he had been in the trenches; and how beautiful it was to remember—as she did suddenly, and not irrelevantly, she knew, though she could not trace the relevance—that, in the little volume, written since his return, there had not been a shadow of the ugly rancour, revengeful and provocative, one met in some other soldier-poets whom one might have fancied to be of his kind. For how he must have hated it! And, at the same time,—memory brought back a line, a stanza here and there, from her snatched reading—how holy he had found it; seeing so much more than error, death, and suffering.

Her eyes dwelt on him with something beyond the kindly wish to spare him as she said, "Please sit down. You must be very tired and you are not strong, Rhoda told me. Don't be afraid of me. I am an old lady who can listen to anything and, I think, understand a great deal. I've already heard a great deal from Rhoda. I'm anything but unfriendly to you, I assure you."

It was—she was aware of it when it had crossed her lips—a curious thing to say to her niece's lover, to the man who had destroyed Tim's happiness and wrecked Niel's home; but it was too true not to be said. And she was perfectly sure now that it was not Mr. Darley who had wrecked and destroyed. It was Rhoda who had taken him, of course; not he Rhoda. He would never take anybody. He would stand and gaze at them as he now gazed at her, and only when they threw out appealing arms would he move towards them. Rhoda had thrown out appealing arms—after she discovered that alluring arms had no effect. Mrs. Delafield's impressions and intuitions tumbled forth in positive clusters as she took in her companion. Allurements, Russian-ballet back-grounds, snowy throats and velvet eyes, would have no effect upon him at all; he cared as little about them at one end of the scale of sensations as about rats and corpses at the other. He would not even see them. It was something else he had seen in Rhoda; something she had found herself driven to display. And if she were getting tired of him already, it was simply because, having trapped him with the artifice, she now found herself shut up with him in a cage, which, while it was of her own making, was extremely uncongenial to her.

Mr. Darley was far too absorbed in what she had just said to him to think of taking the chair. It had helped him incalculably—that was quite apparent; for though the blush stayed, and though he was still wild and shy, they had already, indubitably, begun to understand each other.

"Do you mean," he asked, "not unfriendly to me or not unfriendly to Rhoda?"

This was an unexpected question, and for a moment, not knowing what it portended, she hardly knew how to meet it. But the understanding that seemed to deepen with every moment made truth the most essential thing, and she replied after only a hesitation, "To you."

Mr. Darley looked all his astonishment. "But why? Do you feel that you like me, too? Because, of course, I've never forgotten you. That's why I felt it possible to come to-day."

And since truth was essential, it was she, now, who looked, with her surprise, something that she felt to be a recognition, as she replied, "I suppose it must be that. I suppose we liked each other at first sight. I certainly didn't know the feeling was reciprocal."

"Nor did I!" Mr. Darley exclaimed. He took the chair at the other end of the hearthrug, facing her, his knees crossed, his arms clutched tightly across his chest; and now he was able to reach his journey's goal. As all, on Rhoda's side, had been made clear to her that morning, so on his, all was clear, as he said, with a solemnity so young, so genuine that it almost brought tears to her eyes, "Then since you do like me, please don't let her leave me!"

The situation was before her, definite and overpowering; but how it could have come about remained veiled like the misty approaches to a mountain.

"Does Rhoda want to leave you?" she questioned.

"Why—didn't you know?" Mr. Darley's face flashed with a sort of stupor. "Didn't she come for that?"

"You answer my questions first," Mrs. Delafield said after a moment.

He was obedient and full of trust. "It's because of the child, you know, that lovely little creature in London. From the first—you can't think how long ago it already seems, though we have hardly been a week together—I've seen it growing, that feeling in her that she couldn't bear it. Other things, too; but that more than all. At least," he was truthful to the last point of scruple, "I think so. And though she did not tell me that she was saying good-bye this morning, I knew—I knew—that she was coming to you because she wanted her child, and would accept anything, endure anything, to be with it again."

"What do you think Rhoda had to endure?" Mrs. Delafield inquired.

"Oh—you can't ask me that! I saw you in it and you saw me!" Mr. Darley exclaimed. "You will be straight with me? You saw that soulless life of hers, with that selfish figurehead of a husband for all guide. She was suffocating in it. She didn't need to tell me. I saw it in her face before she told me. How can a woman live with a man she doesn't love? When you said not unfriendly to me, did you mean to make a difference? Did you mean that you don't care for Rhoda? Yet she's always loved and trusted you, she told me, more than any one. You were the one reality she clung to. That's why she could come to you to-day."

"What I mean is that I'm on your side, not on Rhoda's," said Mrs. Delafield, and at the moment her charming old white face expressed, perhaps as never before in her life, the quality of decisiveness. "I am on your side. But I have to see what that is."

He was feeling her face even more than her words. He was gazing at her with a rapt scrutiny which, she reflected, exonerating Rhoda to that extent, would make it difficult for a woman receiving such a tribute not to wish to retain it permanently. It enriched and sustained one and—although it was strange that she should feel this—troubled and moved one, too. A sense of pain stirred in her, and of wonder about herself and her fitness to receive such gazes. One really couldn't, at sixty-three, have growing pains; yet Mr. Darley's gaze filled her with that troubled consciousness of expanding life. He wanted Rhoda. She wanted Jane Amoret. So, wasn't it all right? Wasn't she all right? His side was her side. They wanted the same thing. But the troubled sap of the new consciousness was rising in her.

"My side is really Rhoda's side," said Mr. Darley, as if answering her thought. He held his knee in gripped hands and spoke with rapid security. He was still shy, but he now knew exactly what he wished to say, and how to say it. "It's Rhoda's side, if only she'd see it. That's why I was not disloyal in asking my question when you said you weren't unfriendly. Really—really—you will believe me—it's for her, too. I wouldn't have let her come with me if it hadn't been. I'm not so selfish as I seem. I know it's dreadful about the child. But—this is my secret; Rhoda does not guess it and I could never tell her—she doesn't love the child as she thinks she does. Not really. In spite of her longing. She longs to love it, of course; but she isn't a mother; not to that child. That's another reason. It was all false. The whole thing. The whole of her life. The real truth is," said Christopher Darley, gazing large-eyed at her, "that Rhoda is frightened and wants to go back. She's not as brave as she thought she was. Not quite as brave as I thought. But if she yields to her fear and leaves me,—she hasn't yet, I know, I see that in your face—but if she goes back to her old life, it will mean dust, humiliation, imprisonment forever."

"That's what I told her," Mrs. Delafield said, her eyes on his.

"I knew! I knew!" cried the young man. "I knew you'd done something beautiful for me—for us. Because you see the truth. And you were able to succeed where I failed! You were able to convince her! You've saved us both! Oh, how I thank you!"

"It wasn't quite like that," said Mrs. Delafield. "It wasn't to save either of you. I don't think it right for a woman to leave her husband with another man because she has ceased to love her husband. But I made her go back. I wouldn't even let her tell me that she wanted to leave you. I didn't convince her. I merely made it impossible for her. She left me reluctant and bewildered. You haven't found out yet,"—Mrs. Delafield leaned forward and picked up the little poker; the fire needed no poking and the movement expressed only her inner restlessness,—"you haven't found out that Rhoda, at all events, is very selfish?"

Christopher Darley at that stopped short. "Oh, yes, I have," he answered then; but the frightened croak was in his voice as he said it.

"And have you found out, too," said Mrs. Delafield, eyeing her poker, sparing him, giving him time, "that she's unscrupulous and cold-hearted? Do you see the sort of life she'll make for you, if she is faithful to you and stays with you, not because she's faithful, not because she wants to stay, but gagged and baulked by me? Haven't you already—yourself, been a little frightened sometimes?" she finished.

She kept her eyes on her poker and gave Mr. Darley his time, and indeed he needed it.

"If you've been so wonderful," he said at last, with the slow care of one who threads his way among swords; "if, though you think we're lawbreakers, you think, too, that we've made ourselves another law and are bound to stand by it; if you've sent her back to me—why do you ask me that? But no," he went on, "I'm not frightened. You see—I love her."

"She doesn't love you," said Mrs. Delafield.

"She will! She will!"—It made Mrs. Delafield think of the shaking heart-throbs of the blackbird.—"All that you see,—yes, yes, I won't pretend to you, because I trust you as I've never before trusted any human being, because you are truer than any one I've ever met,—it's all true. She is all that. But don't you see further? Don't you see it's the life? She's never known anything else. She's never had a chance."

"She's known me. She's had me."

Mrs. Delafield's eyes did not leave the poker. But under the quiet statement the struggle in her reached its bitter close. She had lost Jane Amoret. She must give her up. Not for her sake; nor for Rhoda's,—oh, in no sense for Rhoda's,—but for his. She could not let him pay the price. She must save him from Rhoda.

"What do you mean?" he asked; and it was as if crumbling before her secure strength, almost with tears.

"I mean that you'll never make anything different of her. I never have, and I've known her since she was born. You won't make her, and she'll unmake you. She is disintegrating. She has always been like that. Nothing has spoiled her. From the first she's been selfish and untender. I don't mean to say that she hasn't good points. She has a sense of humour; and she's honest with herself: she knows what she wants and why she wants it—although she may take care that you don't. She isn't petty or spiteful or revengeful. No,"—Mrs. Delafield moved her poker slowly up and down as she carved it out for him, and it seemed to be into her own heart she was cutting,—"there is a largeness and a dignity about Rhoda. But she feels no beauty and no tragedy in life, only irony and opportunity. You'll no more change her than you'll change a flower, a fish, or a stone."

Holding his knee in the strained grasp, Christopher Darley kept his eyes on her, breathing quickly.

"Why did she come with me, then?" he asked, after the silence between them had grown long. (Strange, she thought, so near they were, that he could not know her heart was breaking, too. All the time it was Jane Amoret's sleeping eyelashes she saw.) "Why did she love me? I am not irony or opportunity."

"Do you think she ever loved you?" said Mrs. Delafield. "Was it not only that she wanted you to love her? Wasn't it because you were different, and difficult, and new? I think so. I think you found her at a bored, antagonistic moment; money-quarrels with her husband,—he is a good young fellow, Niel, and he used to worship her,—the war over and life to take up again on terms already stale. She is calculating; but she is adventurous and reckless, too. So she went. And of course she was in love with you then. That goes without saying, and you'll know what I mean by it. But Rhoda gets through things quickly. She has no soil in her in which roots can grow; perhaps that's what I mean by saying she can't change. One can't, if one can't grow roots. But now you are no longer new or difficult. You are easy and old—already old; and she's tired of you. You bore her. You constrain and baffle her—if she's to keep up appearances with you at all; and she'd like to do that, because she admires you exceedingly. So she wants to go back to Niel. I know," said Mrs. Delafield, slightly shaking her poker, "that if I'd given her a loophole this morning, she'd be on her way to London now."

"And why didn't you?" asked Christopher Darley.

Ah, why? Again she brooded over the softly breathing little profile, again met the upward gaze of Jane Amoret's grey eyes. Well might he ask why. But there was the one truth she could not give him. There was another that she could, and she had it ready. "I hadn't seen you," she said.

"You thought it right for her to come back to me, until you saw me?"

"I thought it beneath her dignity—as I said to her—to be unfaithful to two men within a fortnight."

"But why should you care for her dignity?" Mr. Darley strangely pressed. "Why shouldn't you care more for your brother's dignity, and her husband's, and her child's—all the things she said you'd care for?"

He had brought her eyes to his now, and, for the first time since they met, it was he who had the advantage. Frowning, yet clear, he bent his great young eyes upon her and she knew, dismayingly, that her thoughts were scattered.

"I have always cared for Rhoda." She seized the first one. "Is it a future for Rhoda to disintegrate the life of the man who loves her and to get no good of him? Isn't it better for a woman like Rhoda to go back to the apparent dignity, since she has no feeling for the real? Isn't that what you would have felt, if you'd been feeling for Rhoda? It wasn't because you felt for her," said Christopher Darley. "You had some other reason. You are keeping another reason from me. You know," he urged upon her with a strange, still austerity, "you know you can't do that. You know we must say the truth to each other. You know that we simply belong to each other, you and I."

"My dear Mr. Darley—my dear young man!"

She was, indeed, bereft of all resource. She laid down her poker and, as she did so, felt herself disarming before him. His eyes, following her retreat, challenged her, almost with fierceness.

"I know—I know that you are giving up something because of me," he said. "You want her to go back to her husband now, so that I may be free. It wasn't of me you thought this morning; nor of your brother, nor of Rhoda. Everything changed for you after you saw me. What is it? What is it that made you send Rhoda back to me and that makes you now want to free me? You are beautiful—but you are terrible. You do beautiful and terrible things. And you must let me share. You must let me decide, too, if you do them for me!"

He had started up, but not to come nearer in his appeal and his demand. Cut to the heart as he was,—for she knew how she had pierced,—it was rather the probing of some more intolerable pain that moved him. And looking down at her with eyes intolerant of her mercy, he embodied to her her sense of a new life and a new conscience. Absurd though his words might seem, they were true. Though never, perhaps, again to meet, she and Christopher Darley recognized in each other some final affinity and owed each other final truth.

She no longer felt old and wise, but young and helpless before the compulsion of the kindred soul. She owed him the truth, and in giving it she must risk his freedom and his happiness. Looking up at him, that sense of compulsion upon her, she said, "It was because of Jane Amoret. It was because I loved her and wanted to keep her."

Christopher Darley grew paler than before. "She is here?"

"Yes. She came this morning. She is upstairs, sleeping."

"Rhoda saw her?"

"Yes."

"And left her? To you?"

"Yes. Left her to me."

He raised his head with a backward jerk and stared out of the window before him. She kept her eyes on his face, measuring its strength against hers. He was not measuring. He seemed to be seeing the beautiful and terrible things of which, he had told her, she was capable. She felt, when his eyes came back to her, that he had judged her.

"You see you can't," he said gently.

"Can't what? Can't keep her, you mean, of course."

"Anything but that. You can't abandon her—even for my sake."

So that had been the judgment. He saw only beauty. "I shan't abandon her. I shall always be able to see as much of her as I did of Rhoda, and more. And she is different from Rhoda. I shan't have the special joy of her, but I shall have the good."

"Moreover," he went on, with perfect gentleness, putting her words aside, "I can't abandon Rhoda. All that you have said is true. But it doesn't go far enough. You yourself, you know, see life too much in terms of irony, of fact rather than faith. You've owned that Rhoda is adventurous and honest;

you've owned that she doesn't lie to herself. Then she has growth in her. No human being can be like a flower or a fish or a stone. It was mere literature, your saying that. Every human being has futures and futures within it. You know it really. Why you yourself, though you are so old and fixed, are different now from what you were an hour ago. I am different, of course. And Rhoda will be different, too. She won't disintegrate me. She'll make me very miserable, doubtless; she has already. And I shall make her angry. But I shall hold her, and she'll change. You shall see. I promise you. And you will keep Jane Amoret, and she will be eternally different because of you."

Mrs. Delafield, while he spoke, had risen. She stood before him, grasping her gold chain on either side, her eyes very nearly level with his, and she summoned all her will, her strength, her wisdom to meet him. Yes, they had come to that, she and this boy.

"I accept all your faith," she said. "Only you must help me to make my world, and not yours, with it. Don't be afraid for Jane Amoret. I shall be firmly in her life. Rhoda shan't keep me out. She won't want to keep me out. Rhoda has far more chance of changing, of learning something from this experience, as a disconcerted and forgiven wife than as a sullen adventuress; and you—you will not be miserable; not with Rhoda, at all events; and you will be free. I am going to send a wire to Rhoda, at once, and tell her that I have reconsidered my advice to her. That, in itself, will show her how I managed her this morning. I shall tell her that she must go to London to-night, to her father. And to-morrow I'll take Jane Amoret up and bring Rhoda and Niel together."

He took it all in, wide-eyed, he too now measuring the threat.

"You can't," he said; "I won't let you!"

"You'll have to let me. I have the fact on my side as well as the faith. She wants to leave you. She wants only the excuse of being asked. You can't stop my giving her the excuse." Yes, after all, her fact against his faith, she must have her way. What could his love for Rhoda and his feeling for herself do against the ironic fact that Rhoda, simply, was tired of him? "You must see that you can't force her to stay," she said. "You couldn't even prevent her coming to me this morning."

She looked at him with all the force of her advantage and saw that before the cruel fact, and her determination, he knew his helplessness. It was, again, the bird arrested in its impulse; and a veil seemed to fall across his face, a shyness, almost a wildness to shut them out from each other. He dropped his eyes before her.

"Dear Mr. Darley, my dear young friend, see that it's best. See that it's best all round. See it with me," she begged. "I was wrong this morning; wrong from the very first. Let it come to that only. Count yourself out. It was of myself, of my own delight in the child that I was thinking. No, not even thinking; I tried to think it was for her; but it was my own feeling that decided. If you had never come, it would still have been right to give her up—though I should never have seen it unless you'd come. It was almost a crime that I committed. They had asked me to implore her to go back; they trusted me. And I prevented the message coming to her. I did not believe the things I said to her—not as she thought I believed them. I did not care a rap about her dignity; you saw the falsity at once. I cared only about keeping Jane Amoret."

He stood there before her, remote, unmoved, with downcast, unanswering eyes.

"Are you angry? Don't you see it, too?" she pleaded.

"No." He shook his head. "You had a right to keep the child."

"Against all those other reasons? Against my own conscience?"

"Yes. Because you were strong enough. You were right, because you were strong enough. I believe in law, too, you see—unless one is strong enough to break it for something better. You were. It was a beautiful thing to do."

"But then, if you think me so strong, why not trust me now? This, now, is the thing I want to do."

"Because of me. It isn't against the law you are acting now; it's against your own life. I am not angry. But it crushes me."

They stood there then, she deeply meditating, he fixed in his unyielding grief, for how long she could not have said. Parton's step outside broke in upon their mute opposition.

VI

SHE and Mr. Darley, Mrs. Delafield was aware, presented precisely the abstracted, alienated air that Parton would expect. The young man moved away to the window while she took from the salver the note Parton presented. Then, her hand arrested in the very act by a recognition,

"Is there an answer?" she asked.

"No answer, ma'am."

"Who brought it?"

"A man from the station, ma'am."

"Very well, Parton."

Parton was gone. Mr. Darley kept his back turned. She held the note in her hand and stared at it. The writing was Rhoda's; the envelope one of the station-master's. She had been at the station, then, when she wrote, four miles away. The London train, for which she had been waiting, had gone long since; it had gone before the arrival of Mr. Darley's.

An almost overpowering presage rose in her mind; she could hardly, for a moment, summon the decision with which to open the envelope. Then, reading as she stood, she felt the blood flow up to her face.

For it was almost too much, although it was, through Rhoda's act, she who had won finally. Even she, then, had not yet correctly measured Rhoda's irony or Rhoda's sardonic assurance. Rhoda, after all, did not care to keep up appearances with her, and, after all, why should she? Here was fact, and it had been fact all through. She wanted most to go back. She wanted it more than to be dignified in her aunt's eyes, or, really, in anybody else's. Once back Rhoda would take care of her dignity. In a flash Mrs. Delafield saw how little, when all was said and done, Rhoda would pay.

DEAR AUNT ISABEL [she wrote, in her ample, tranquil hand]: I've been thinking over all you said and have come to the conclusion that you are considering me too much. I feel that I must consider my child. I have made a grave mistake and am not too proud to own it. Christopher and I are not at all fitted to make each other happy. So I have wired to father that I arrive this afternoon, and to Niel that I will see him to-morrow. I have written too, of course, to my poor Christopher. But he will understand me. Thank you so much, dear Aunt Isabel, for your kindness and helpfulness.

Your affectionate RHODA

P.S. Will you send nurse up with Jane Amoret within the week? Not at once, please; that would look rather foolish.

With the accumulated weight of absurdity, relief, dismay, she had sunk down into her chair, still gazing at the letter, and it was dismay that grew. As if with a violent jolt back to earth, Rhoda seemed to show her that life was not docile to nobilities. She hated to think that he must feel with her that shattering fall. There was nothing for them to do now for each other; no contest and no sacrifice. Rhoda had settled everything.

She spoke to him at last, and, as he came to her, not looking around at him, she held out the note. He stood behind her to read it; and after that he did not speak.

She heard him move presently, vaguely, and then, vaguely, he drifted to and fro. He walked here and there; he paused, no doubt to feel his bones and to count how many had been broken, and then, with a start, he went on again.

"Please come where I can see you," she said at last.

He came at once, obediently, standing as he had stood a little while ago before the fire, his hands locked behind him, but now with face bent down, fixed in its effort to see clearly what had happened to them.

"You see, it was over. You see, you couldn't have made anything of it." It was almost with tears that she besought him not to suffer too much. "You have nothing to regret, except having believed in her. Tell me that you are not too unhappy."

"I don't know what I am," Christopher said. "But I know I've more to regret than having believed in her. I've all the folly and mischief I've made." He had thought it out and she could not deny what he had seen, not even when he went on, "If it could have been in our way,—yours and mine, or, at least, what was yours this morning, when you thought you had kept her with me,—everything might have been atoned for. It might have meant a certain kind of beauty, and a certain kind of happiness, even, perhaps. But in this way, the way she's chosen, it only means just that—folly, mischief,"—he turned to the fire and looked down into it,—"sin," he finished.

She could not deny it, even to give him comfort; but she could find something else. "It was Rhoda who chose. You, whatever your mistakes, chose very differently. I'm not trying to shift responsibility; to make mistakes is to be foolish and mischievous. But can't even sin be atoned for? Doesn't it all now depend on you? That you should make yourself worth it. You are the only one of us who can do that."

He turned to her and his eyes studied her with an unaccepting gentleness.

"You mean because I'm a poet? It isn't like you, really, to say that. You don't believe in poets and their mission in that sense. It's too facile."

"Not only because you are a poet. I wasn't thinking so much of that, although your gift helps. But simply because you are young and good."

"I'm not good enough," said Christopher. "And I'm too young. You've shown me that. I am afraid of myself. I see what one can do while meaning the best."

She watched him with grave tenderness, feeling again, in his dispassionate capacity for accepted experience, his strange maturity. And knowing all that might be difficult, yet knowing that it would be, after all, to a decision like her own, the merest gossamers of convention that she must brave, she said,—and as she looked up at him his face seemed to blend with the face of her little, sleeping, lost Jane Amoret,—"Don't you think I, perhaps, could be of help, while you are so young?"

He did not understand her at all. He, too, was absorbed in his inner image of loss, yet he, too, was almost as aware of her as she of him, and his eyes, with their austere gentleness, dwelt on her, as if treasuring, of this last encounter, his completed vision of her.

"Yes, you will be. I shall never forget you and what you've been to me. I'll do my best," he promised her. "But I seem to have lost everything. I could be strong for her; I don't know that I can be strong enough for myself."

"That's what I mean," said Mrs. Delafield. "It takes years to be strong enough for one's self, and even when one's old one hasn't sometimes learned how to be. I'm not sure, after this morning, that I've learned yet. But I know that I could be strong for you. Will you let me try? Will you let me take care of you a little and guard you from the Rhodas until the right person comes?"

"What do you mean?" he asked; and, answering the look in her face, tears sprang to his eyes.

"We belong to each other. Didn't you say it?" she smiled. "We are friends. We ought not to lose each other now."

"Oh! But—" He gazed at her. "How could you! After what I've done!"

"You've done nothing that makes me like you less."

"Oh—I can't! I can't!" said Christopher Darley. "How could I accept it from you? Already you've been unbelievably beautiful to me. It's not as if you were a Bohemian sort of creature, like me. Appearances must count for you. And the appearance of being friends with your niece's discarded lover—no—I can't see it for you. I can imagine you being above the law, but I can't imagine you being above appearances. I don't think that I should want you to be. I care about appearances, too, when they are yours."

It crossed her mind, with almost a mirthful sense of the sort of appearances she would have to deal with, that Parton's face would be worth watching. Poor Tim's hovered more grievously in the background. But, after all, it would be a Tim with wounds well salved.

"It's just because mine are so secure and recognized, don't you see, that I can do what I like with them," she said. "It's not for me a question of appearances, but of realities. After all, my dear young man, what am I going to get out of it all? My roots have been torn up too, you know."

"Because of me! Because of me!" Christopher groaned. "Do you think you need remind me of that? Shall I ever forgive myself for it? Get out of it? You'll get nothing. You've been tormented between us all, and you lose Jane Amoret."

"Then don't let me lose you too," said Mrs. Delafield.

Again, with the tears, his blush sprang to his face, and he stood there incredulous, looking down at her, almost as helpless in the shyness the unexpected gift brought upon him as he had been when he first came in to her.

"Really you mean it?" he murmured. "Really I can do something for you, too? Because, unless I can, I couldn't accept it."

"You can make me much less lonely, when she's gone," said Mrs. Delafield.

She knew that this was to give the gift in such a way as to ensure its acceptance; but he murmured, stung again intolerably by the thought of Jane Amoret, "Oh—I can't bear it for you!"

"You can help me to bear it."

Still he pressed upon her what he saw as her sacrifice. "You mean that I may see you when I like? I may always write and you'll always answer? I can sometimes, even, come and stay, like any other friend? Please realize that if you let me come down on you like that, I may come hard. I'm frightfully lonely, too."

"As hard as you like. I want you to come hard. Like any friend. Yes."

She was smiling up at the young man, and, as she had promised herself years for Jane Amoret, she promised herself now years—though not so many would be needed—for Christopher Darley. It was in the thought of what she could do for Christopher Darley that she saw Rhoda's punishment. Not for having left him, but for having taken him; for not having known what to do with him without taking him. And Rhoda would see it with her, if no one else did.

"Come, you must quite believe in me," she said. "Give me your hand, dear Christopher, and tell me that you take this meddling, commanding old woman to be your friend."

He had no words as he took the hand she gave him, but from his look it might have been as if he at last received into his keeping the great gift, the precious casket of the future; and his eyes, like those of a devout young knight, dedicated themselves to her service.

It was again gift and miracle; and though in her mind was the thought of all her mournings, and of the lost Jane Amoret, she felt, rooting itself in the darkness and sorrow, yet another flower.

"And now," she said, for they must not both begin to cry, "please ring the bell for me. The time has not quite come for your first visit; but, before you go, we will have our first tea together."

HEPATICAS

I

OTHER people's sons were coming home for the three or four days' leave. The first gigantic struggle—furious onslaught and grim resistance—was over. Paris, pale, and slightly shuddering still, stood safe. Calais was not taken, and, dug into their trenches, it was evident that the opposing armies would lie face to face with no decisive encounter possible until the spring.

There was, with all their beauty and terror, an element of the facetious in these unexpected holidays, of the matter-of-factness, the freedom from strain or sentiment that was the English oddity and the English strength. Men who had known the horrors of the retreat from Mons or the carnage of Ypres, who had not taken off their clothes for ten days at a stretch or slept for four nights, came home from trenches knee-deep in mud, from battlefields heaped with unburied dead, and appeared immaculate and cheerful at breakfast; a little sober and preoccupied, perhaps; touched, perhaps, with strangeness; but ready for the valorous family jest, and alluding to the war as if, while something too solemn for adequate comment, it were yet something that lent itself to laughter. One did such funny things, and saw them; of the other things one did not speak; and there was the huge standing joke of an enemy who actually hated one. These grave and cheerful young men hated nobody; but they were very eager to go back again; and they were all ready, not only to die but to die good-humouredly. From the demeanour of mothers and wives and sisters it was evident that nothing would be said or done to make this readiness difficult; but Mrs. Bradley, who showed serenity to the world and did not even when alone allow herself to cry, suspected that the others, beneath their smiles, carried hearts as heavy with dread as her own.

It had been heavy, with hope now as well as with dread, for the past week. It was a week since she had last heard from Jack. Mrs. Crawley over the hill, had had a wire, and her husband was now with her; and Lady Wrexham expected her boy to-morrow. There was no certainty at all as regarded herself; yet at any moment she might have her wire; and feeling to-day the stress of waiting too great to be borne in passivity, she left her books and letters and put on her gardening shoes and gloves and went out to her borders.

For weeks now the incessant rain had made the relief and solace of gardening almost an impossibility; but to-day was mild and clear. There was no radiance in the air; curtains of pearly mist shut out the sky; yet here and there a soft opening in the white showed a pale, far blue, gentle and remote as the gaze of a wandering goddess, and the hills seemed to smile quietly up at the unseen sun. Mrs. Bradley, as she went along the river-path, could look across at the hills; the river-path and the hills were the great feature of Dorrington,—the placid, comely red brick house to which she and Jack had come fifteen years ago, after the death of her husband in India. Enclosed by woods, and almost catching sight of the road,—from its upper windows and over its old brick wall,—the house would have seemed to her too commonplace and almost suburban, in spite of the indubitably old oak-panelling of the drawing-room, had it not been for the river and the hills. Stepping out on to the lawn from the windows of the drawing-room, she and Jack, on that April day, had found themselves confronting both—the limpid, rapid little stream, spanned near the house by its mossy bridge, and the hills, beyond the meadows, streaked with purple woodlands and rising, above the woods, to slopes russet, fawn, and azure. Jack, holding her by the hand, had pointed at once with an eager "Isn't it pretty, mummy!"—even at eight he had cared almost as much as she, and extraordinarily in the same way, for the sights of the country; and if the hills hadn't settled the question, it was settled, quite finally, ten minutes later, by the white hepaticas.

They had come upon them suddenly, after their tour of the walled kitchen garden and their survey of the lawn with its ugly shrubberies,—now long forgotten,—penetrating a thicket of hazels and finding themselves in an opening under trees where neighbouring woods looked at them over an old stone wall, and where, from an old stone bench, one could see the river. The ground was soft with the fallen leaves of many an autumn; a narrow path ran, half obliterated, down to the river; and among the faded brown, everywhere, rose the thick clusters, the dark leaves, and the snowy flowers,—poignant, amazing in their beauty.

She and Jack had stopped short to gaze. She had never before seen such white hepaticas, or so many, or so placed. And Jack, presently, lifting his dear nut-brown head and nut-brown eyes, had said, gazing up at her as he had gazed at the flowers, "They are just like you, mummy."

She had felt at once that they were like her; more like than the little boy's instinct could grasp. He had thought of the darkness and whiteness; her widow's weeds and pale face had suggested that; but he could not know the sorrow, the longing, the earthly sense of irreparable loss, the heavenly sense of a possession unalterably hers, that the dark, melancholy leaves and celestial whiteness of the flowers expressed to her. Tears had risen to her eyes and she had stooped and kissed her child,—how like her husband's that little face!—and had said, after a moment, "We must never leave them, Jack."

They had never left them. Dorrington had been their home for fifteen years, and the hepaticas the heart of it. It had always seemed to them both the loveliest ritual of the year, that early spring one when, in the hazel copse, they would find the white hepaticas again in flower. And of all the garden labours none were sweeter than those that cherished and divided and protected the beloved flowers.

Mrs. Bradley, to-day, worked in her long border, weeding, forking, placing belated labels. She was dressed in black, her straw hat bound beneath her chin by a ribbon and her soft gardening gloves rolling back from her firm, white wrists. Her gestures expressed a calm energy, an accurate grace. She was tall, and when she raised herself to look over the meadows at the hills, she showed small, decisive features, all marked, in the pallor of her face, as if with the delicate, neutral emphasis of an etching: the grey, scrutinizing eyes, the charming yet ugly nose, the tranquil mouth that had, at the corners, a little fall, half sweet, half bitter, as if with tears repressed or a summoned smile. Squared at brow and chin, it would, but for the mildness of the gaze, have been an imperious face; and her head, its whitened hair drawn back and looped in wide braids behind, had an air at once majestic and unworldly.

She had worked for over an hour and the last label was set beside a precious clump of iris. The hazel copse lay near by; and gathering up her tools, drawing off her wet gloves, she followed the path under the leafless branches and among the hepatica leaves to the stone bench, where, sinking down, she knew that she was very tired. She could see, below the bank, the dark, quick stream; a pale, diffused light in the sky showed where the sun was dropping toward the hills.

Where was Jack at this moment, this quiet moment of a monotonous English winter day?—so like the days of all the other years that it was impossible to think of what was happening a few hours' journey away across the Channel. Impossible to think of it; yet the thick throb of her heart spoke to the full of its significance. She had told herself from the beginning— passionate, rebellious creature as, at bottom, she knew herself to be, always in need of discipline and only in these later years schooled to a control and submission that, in her youth, she would have believed impossible to her— she had told herself, when he had gone from her, that, as a soldier's widow, she must see her soldier son go to death. She must give him to that; be ready for it; and if he came back to her it would be as if he were born again, a gift, a grace, unexpected and unclaimed. She must feel, for herself as well as for her country, that these days of dread were also days of a splendour and beauty unmatched by any in England's history, and that a soldier's widow must ask for no more glorious fate for her son than death in such a cause. She had told herself all this many times; yet, as she sat there, her hands folded on her lap, her eyes on the stream below, she felt that she was now merely motherhood, tense, huddled, throbbing and longing, longing for its child.

Then, suddenly, she heard Jack's footsteps. They came, quick and light, along the garden path; they entered the wood; they were near, but softened by the fallen leaves. And, half rising, afraid of her own joy, she hardly knew that she saw him before she was in his arms; and it was better to meet thus, in the blindness and darkness of their embrace, her cheek pressed against his hair, his head buried close between her neck and shoulder.

"Jack!—Jack!" she heard herself say.

He said nothing, holding her tightly to him, with quick breaths; and even after she had opened her eyes and could look down at him,—her own, her dear, beautiful Jack,—could see the nut-brown head, the smooth brown cheek, the firm brown hand which grasped her, he did not for a long time raise his head and look at her. When, at last, he did look up, she could not tell, through her tears, whether, like herself, he was trying to smile.

They sat down together on the bench. She did not ask him why he had not wired. That question pressed too sharply on her heart; to ask might seem to reproach.

"Darling—you are so thin,—so much older,— but you look—strong and well."

"We're all of us extraordinarily fit, mummy. It's wholesome, living in mud."

"And wholesome living among bursting shells? I had your last letter telling of that miraculous escape."

"There have been a lot more since then. Every day seems a miracle—that one's alive at the end of it."

"But you get used to it?"

"All except the noise. That always seems to daze me still. Some of our fellows are deaf from it.—You heard of Toppie, mother?" Jack asked.

Toppie was Alan Graham, Jack's nearest friend. He had been killed ten days before.

"I heard it, Jack. Were you with him?"

"Yes. It was in a bayonet charge. He didn't suffer. A bullet went right through him. He just gave a little cry and fell." Jack's voice had the mildness of a sorrow that has passed beyond the capacity for emotion. "We found him afterwards. He is buried out there."

"You must tell Frances about it, Jack. I went to her at once." Frances was Toppie's sister. "She is bearing it so bravely."

"I must write to her. She would be sure to be plucky."

He answered all her questions, sitting closely against her, his arm around her; looking down, while he spoke, and twisting, as had always been his boyish way, a button on her coat. He was at that enchanting moment of young manhood when the child is still apparent in the man. His glance was shy yet candid; his small, firm lips had a child's gravity. With his splendid shoulders, long legs, and noble little head, he was yet as endearing as he was impressive. His mother's heart ached with love and pride and fear as she gazed at him.

And a question came, near the sharp one, yet hoping to evade it:—

"Jack, dearest, how long will you be with me? How long is the leave?"

He raised his eyes then and looked at her; a curious look. Something in it blurred her mind with a sense of some other sort of fear.

"Only till to-night," he said.

It seemed confusion rather than pain that she felt. "Only till to-night, Jack? But Richard Crawley has been back for three days already. I thought they gave you longer?"

"I know, mummy." His eyes were dropped again and his hand at the button—did it tremble?—twisted and untwisted. "I've been back for three days already.—I've been in London."

"In London?" Her breath failed her. The sense of alien fear became a fog, horrible, suffocating. "But—Jack—why?"

"I didn't wire, mummy, because I knew I'd have to be there for most of my time. I felt I couldn't wire and tell you. I felt I had to see you when I told you. Mother—I'm married.—I came back to get married.—I was married this morning.—Oh, mother, can you ever forgive me?"

His shaking hands held her and his eyes could not meet hers.

She felt the blood rush, as if her heart had been divided with a sword, to her throat, to her eyes, choking her, burning her; and as if from far away she heard her own voice saying, after a little time had passed, "There's nothing I couldn't forgive you, Jack. Tell me. Don't be afraid of hurting me."

He held her tightly, still looking down as he said, "She is a dancer, mother, a little dancer. It was in London, last summer. A lot of us came up from Aldershot together. She was in the chorus of one of those musical comedies. Mother, you can never understand. But it wasn't just low and vulgar. She was so lovely,—so very young,—with the most wonderful golden hair and the sweetest eyes.—I don't know.—I simply went off my head when I saw her. We all had supper together afterwards. Toppie knew one of the other girls, and Dollie was there. That's her name—Dollie Vaughan—her stage name. Her real name was Watson. Her people, I think, were little tradespeople, and she'd lost her father and mother, and an aunt had been very unkind. She told me all about it that night. Mother, please believe just this: it wasn't only the obvious thing.—I know I can't explain. But you remember, when we read War and Peace"—his broken voice groped for the analogy—"You remember Natacha, when she falls in love with Anatole, and nothing that was real before seems real, and she is ready for anything.—It was like that. It was all fairyland, like that. No one thought it wrong. It didn't seem wrong. Everything went together."

She had gathered his hand closely in hers and she sat there, quiet, looking at her hopes lying slain before her. Her Jack. The wife who was, perhaps, to have been his. The children that she, perhaps, should have seen. All dead. The future blotted out. Only this wraith-like present; only this moment of decision; Jack and his desperate need the only real things left.

And after a moment, for his labouring breath had failed, she said, "Yes, dear?" and smiled at him.

He covered his face with his hands. "Mother, I've ruined your life."

He had, of course, in ruining his own; yet even at that moment of wreckage she was able to remember, if not to feel, that life could mend from terrible wounds, could marvellously grow from compromises and defeats. "No, dearest, no," she said. "While I have you, nothing is ruined. We shall see what can be done. Go on. Tell me the rest."

He put out his hand to hers again and sat now a little turned away from her, speaking on in his deadened, bitter voice.

"There wasn't any glamour after that first time. I only saw her once or twice again. I was awfully sorry and ashamed over the whole thing. Her company left London, on tour, and then the war came, and I simply forgot all about her. And the other day, over there, I had a letter from her. She was in terrible trouble. She was ill and had no money, and no work. And she was going to have a child—my child; and she begged me to send her a little money to help her through, or she didn't know what would become of her."

The fog, the horrible confusion, even the despair, had passed now. The sense of ruin, of wreckage almost irreparable, was there; yet with it, too, was the strangest sense of gladness. He was her own Jack, completely hers, for she saw now why he had done it; she could be glad that he had done it. "Go on, dear," she said. "I understand; I understand perfectly."

"O mother, bless you!" He put her hand to his lips, bowing his head upon it for a moment. "I was afraid you couldn't. I was afraid you couldn't forgive me. But I had to do it. I thought it all over—out there. Everything had become so different after what one had been through. One saw everything differently. Some things didn't matter at all, and other things mattered tremendously. This was one of them. I knew I couldn't just send her money. I knew I couldn't bear to have the poor child born without a name and with only that foolish little mother to take care of it. And when I found I could get this leave, I knew I must marry her. That was why I didn't wire. I thought I might not have time to come to you at all."

"Where is she, Jack?" Her voice, her eyes, her smile at him, showed him that, indeed, she understood perfectly.

"In lodgings that I found for her; nice and quiet, with a kind landlady. She was in such an awful place in Ealing. She is so changed, poor little thing. I should hardly have known her. Mother, darling, I wonder, could you just go and see her once or twice? She's frightfully lonely; and so very young.—If you could.—If you would just help things along a little till the baby comes, I should be so grateful. And, then, if I don't come back, will you, for my sake, see that they are safe?"

"But, Jack," she said, smiling at him, "she is coming here, of course. I shall go and get her to-morrow."

He stared at her and his colour rose. "Get her? Bring her here, to stay?"

"Of course, darling. And if you don't come back, I will take care of them, always."

"But, mother," said Jack, and there were tears in his eyes, "you don't know, you don't realize. I mean—she's; a dear little thing—but you couldn't be happy with her. She'd get most frightfully on your nerves. She's just—just a silly little dancer who has got into trouble."

Jack was clear-sighted. Every vestige of fairyland had vanished. And she was deeply thankful that they should see alike, while she answered, "It's not exactly a time for considering one's nerves, is it, Jack? I hope I shan't get on hers. I must just try and make her as happy as I can."

She made it all seem natural and almost sweet. The tears were in his eyes, yet he had to smile back at her when she said, "You know that I am good at managing people. I'll manage her. And perhaps when you come back, my darling, she won't be a silly little dancer."

They sat now for a little while in silence. While they had talked, a golden sunset, slowly, had illuminated the western sky. The river below them was golden, and the wintry woodlands bathed in light. Jack held her hands and gazed at her. Love could say no more than his eyes, in their trust and sorrow, said to her; she could never more completely possess her son. Sitting there with him, hand in hand, while the light slowly ebbed and twilight fell about them, she felt it to be, in its accepted sorrow, the culminating and transfiguring moment of her maternity.

When they at last rose to go it was the hour for Jack's departure, and it had become almost dark. Far away, through the trees, they could see the lighted windows of the house that waited for them, but to which she must return alone. With his arms around her shoulders, Jack paused a moment, looking about him. "Do you remember that day—when we first came here, mummy?" he asked.

She felt in him suddenly a sadness deeper than any he had yet shown her. The burden of the past she had lifted from him; but he must bear now the burden of what he had done to her, to their life, to all the future. And, protesting against his pain, her mother's heart strove still to shelter him while she answered, as if she did not feel his sadness, "Yes, dear, and do you remember the hepaticas on that day?"

"Like you," said Jack in a gentle voice. "I can hardly see the plants. Are they all right?"

"They are doing beautifully."

"I wish the flowers were out," said Jack. "I wish it were the time for the flowers to be out, so that I could have seen you and them together, like that first day." And then, putting his head down on her shoulder, he murmured, "It will never be the same again. I've spoiled everything for you."

But he was not to go from her uncomforted. She found the firmest voice in which to answer him, stroking his hair and pressing him to her with the full reassurance of her resolution. "Nothing is spoiled, Jack, nothing. You have never been so near me—so how can anything be spoiled? And when you come back, darling, you'll find your son, perhaps; and the hepaticas may be in flower, waiting for you."

II

MRS. BRADLEY and her daughter-in-law sat together in the drawing-room. They sat opposite each other on the two chintz chesterfields placed at right angles to the pleasantly blazing fire, the chintz curtains drawn against a rainy evening. It was a long, low room, with panelled walls; and, like Mrs. Bradley's head, it had an air at once majestic, decorated, and old-fashioned. It was a rather crowded room, with many deep chairs and large couches, many tables with lamps and books and photographs upon them, many porcelains, prints, and pots of growing flowers. Mrs. Bradley, her tea-table before her, was in her evening black silk; lace ruffles rose about her throat; she wore her accustomed necklace of old enamel, blue, black, and white, set with small diamonds, and the enamel locket that had within it Jack's face on one side and his father's on the other; her white hands, moving gently among the teacups, showed an ancient cluster of diamonds above the slender wedding-ring. From time to time she lifted her eyes and smiled quietly over at her daughter-in-law. It was the first time that she had really seen Dollie, that is, in any sense that meant contemplative observation. Dollie had spent her first week at Dorrington in bed, sodden with fatigue rather than ill. "What you need," Mrs. Bradley had said, "is to go to sleep for a fortnight"; and Dollie had almost literally carried out the prescription.

Stealing carefully into the darkened room, with its flowers and open windows and steadily glowing fire, Mrs. Bradley had stood and looked for long moments at all that she could see of her daughter-in-law,—a flushed, almost babyish face lying on the pillow between thick golden braids, sleeping so deeply, so unconsciously,—her sleep making her mother-in-law think of a little boat gliding slowly yet steadily on and on, between new shores; so that, when she was to awake and look about her, it would be as if, with no bewilderment or readjustment, she found herself transformed, a denizen of an altered world. That was what Mrs. Bradley wanted, that Dollie should become an inmate of Dorrington with as little effort or consciousness for any of them as possible, and the drowsy days and nights of infantine slumbers seemed indeed to have brought her very near.

She and Pickering, the admirable woman who filled so skilfully the combined positions of lady's maid and parlourmaid in her little establishment, had braided Dollie's thick tresses, one on either side,—Mrs. Bradley laughing a little and both older women touched, almost happy in their sense of something so young and helpless to take care of. Pickering understood, nearly as well as Jack's mother, that Master Jack, as he had remained to her, had married very much beneath him; but at this time of tragic issues and primitive values, she, nearly as much as Jack's mother, felt only the claim, the pathos of youth and helplessness. It was as if they had a singularly appealing case of a refugee to take care of; social and even moral appraisals were inapplicable to such a case, and Mrs. Bradley felt that she had never so admired Pickering as when seeing that for her, too, they were in abeyance. It was a comfort to feel so fond of Pickering at a time when one was in need of any comfort one could get; and to feel that, creature of codes and discriminations as she was, to a degree that had made her mistress sometimes think of her as a sort of Samurai of service, a function rather than a person, she was even more fundamentally a kind and Christian woman. Between them, cook intelligently sustaining them from below and the housemaids helpful in their degree, they fed and tended and nursed Dollie, and by that eighth day she was more than ready to get up and go down and investigate her new surroundings.

She sat there now, in the pretty tea-gown her mother-in-law had bought for her, leaning back against her cushions, one arm lying along the back of the couch and one foot in its patent-leather shoe, with its sparkling buckle and alarming heel, thrusting forward a carefully arched instep. The attitude made one realize, however completely tenderer preoccupations held the foreground of one's consciousness, how often and successfully she must have sat to theatrical photographers. Her way of smiling, too, very softly, yet with the effect of a calculated and dazzling display of pearly teeth, was impersonal, and directed, as it were, to the public via the camera rather than to any individual interlocutor. Mrs. Bradley even imagined, unversed as she was in the methods of Dollie's world, that of allurement in its conscious and determined sense she was almost innocent. She placed herself, she adjusted her arm and her foot, and she smiled gently; intention hardly went further than that wish to look her best.

Pink and white and gold as she was, and draped there on the chesterfield in a profusion of youth and a frivolity that was yet all passivity, she made her mother-in-law think, and with a certain sinking of the heart, of a Dorothy Perkins rose, a flower she had never cared for; and Dollie carried on the analogy in the sense she gave that there were such myriads more just like her. On almost every page of every illustrated weekly paper, one saw the ingenuous, limpid eyes, the display of eyelash, the lips, their outline emphasized by just that touch of rouge, those copious waves of hair. Like the Dorothy Perkins roses on their pergolas, so these pretty faces seemed—looped, draped, festooned—to climb over all the available spaces of the modern press.

But this, Mrs. Bradley told herself, was to see Dollie with a dry, hard eye, was to see her superficially, from the social rather than from the human point of view. Under the photographic creature must lie the young, young girl,—so young, so harmless that it would be very possible to mould her, with all discretion, all tenderness, into some suitability as Jack's wife. Dollie, from the moment that she had found her, a sodden, battered rose indeed, in the London lodging-house, had shown herself grateful, even humble, and endlessly acquiescent. She had not shown herself at all abashed or apologetic, and that had been a relief; had counted for her, indeed, in her mother-in-law's eyes, as a sort of innocence, a sort of dignity. But if Dollie were contented with her new mother-in-law, and very grateful to her, she was also contented with herself; Mrs. Bradley had been aware of this at once; and she knew now that if she were being carefully and commendingly watched while she poured out the tea, this concentration did not imply unqualified approval. Dollie was the type of young woman to whom she herself stood as the type of the "perfect lady"; but with the appreciation went the proviso of the sharp little London mind,—versed in the whole ritual of smartness as it displayed itself at theatre or restaurant,— that she was a rather dowdy one. She was a lady, perfect but not smart, while, at the same time, the quality of her defect was, she imagined, a little bewildering and therefore a little impressive. Actually to awe Dollie and to make her shy, it would be necessary to be smart; but it was far more pleasant and perhaps as efficacious merely to impress her, and it was as well that Dollie should be impressed; for anything in the nature of an advantage that she could recognize would make it easier to direct, protect, and mould her.

She asked her a good many leisurely and unstressed questions on this first evening, and drew Dollie to ask her others in return; and she saw herself stooping thoughtfully over a flourishing young plant that yet needed transplanting, softly moving the soil about its roots, softly finding out if there were any very deep tap-root that would have to be dealt with. But Dollie, so far as tastes and ideas went, hardly seemed to have any roots at all; so few that it was a question if any change of soil could affect a creature so shallow. She smiled, she was at ease; she showed her complete assurance that a young lady so lavishly endowed with all the most significant gifts, need not occupy herself with mental adornments.

"You're a great one for books, I see," she commented, looking about the room; "I suppose you do a great deal of reading down here to keep from feeling too dull"; and she added that she herself, if there was "nothing doing," liked a good novel, especially if she had a box of sweets to eat while she read it.

"You shall have a box of sweets to-morrow," Mrs. Bradley told her, "with or without the novel, as you like."

And Dollie thanked her, watching her cut the cake, and, as the rain lashed against the windows, remarking on the bad weather and cheerfully hoping that "poor old Jack" wasn't in those horrid trenches. "I think war's a wicked thing, don't you, Mrs. Bradley?" she added.

When Dollie talked in this conventionally solicitous tone of Jack, her mother-in-law could but wish her upstairs again, merely young, merely the tired and battered refugee. She had not much tenderness for Jack, that was evident, nor much imaginativeness in regard to the feelings of Jack's mother. But she soon passed from the theme of Jack and his danger. Her tea was finished and she got up and went to the piano, remarking that there was one thing she could do. "Poor mother used to always say I was made of music. From the time I was a mere tot I could pick out anything on the piano." And placing herself, pressing down the patent-leather shoe on the loud pedal, she surged into a waltz as foolish and as conventionally alluring as her own eyes. Her inaccuracy was equalled only by her facility. Smiling, swaying over the keys with alternate speed and languor, she addressed her audience with altogether the easy mastery of a music-hall artiste: "It's a lovely thing—one of my favourites. I'll often play, Mrs. Bradley, and cheer us up. There is nothing like music for that, is there? it speaks so to the heart." And, whole-heartedly, indeed, she accompanied the melody by a passionate humming.

The piano was Jack's and it was poor Jack who was made of music. How was he to bear it, his mother asked herself, as she sat listening. Dollie, after that initiation, spent many hours at the piano every day,—so many and such noisy hours, that her mother-in-law, unnoticed, could shut herself in the little morning-room that overlooked the brick wall at the front of the house and had the morning sun.

It was difficult to devise other occupations for Dollie. She earnestly disclaimed any wish to have proper music lessons, and when her mother-in-law, patiently persistent, arranged for a skilful mistress to come down twice a week from London, Dollie showed such apathy and dulness that any hope of developing such musical ability as she possessed had to be abandoned. She did not like walking, and the sober pageant of the winter days was a blank book to her. Sewing, she said, had always given her frightful fidgets; and it was with the strangest sense of a privilege, a joy, unhoped-for and now thrust upon her, that Mrs. Bradley sat alone working at the little garments that meant all her future and all Jack's. The baby seemed already more hers than Dollie's.

Sometimes, on a warm afternoon, Dollie, wrapped in her fur cloak, would emerge for a little while and watch her mother-in-law at work in her borders. The sight amused and surprised but hardly interested her, and she soon went tottering back to the house on the preposterous heels that Mrs. Bradley had, as yet, found no means of tactfully banishing. And sometimes, when the piano again resounded, Mrs. Bradley would leave her borders and retreat to the hazel-copse, where, as she sat on the stone bench, she could hear, through the soft sound of the running water, hardly more than the distant beat and hum of Dollie's waltzes; and where, with more and more the sense of escape and safety, she could find a refuge from the sight and sound and scent of Dollie,—the thick, sweet, penetrating scent that was always to be indelibly associated in her mind with this winter of foreboding, of hope, and of growing hopelessness.

In her letters to Jack, she found herself, involuntarily at first, and then deliberately, altering, suppressing, even falsifying. While Dollie had been in bed, when so much hope had been possible of a creature so unrevealed, she had written very tenderly, and she continued, now, to write tenderly, and it was not false to do that; she could feel no hardness or antagonism against poor Dollie. But she continued to write hopefully, as every day hope grew less.

Jack, himself, did not say much of Dollie, though there was always the affectionate message and the affectionate inquiry. But what was difficult to deal with were the hints of his anxiety and fear that stole among the terse, cheerful descriptions of his precarious days. What was she doing with herself? How were she and Dollie getting on? Did Dollie care about any of the things she cared about?

She told him that they got on excellently well, that Dollie spent a good deal of time at the piano, and that when they went out to tea people were perfectly nice and understanding. She knew, indeed, that she could depend on her friends to be that. They accepted Dollie on the terms she asked for her. From friends so near as Mrs. Crawley and Lady Wrexham she had not concealed the fact that Dollie was a misfortune; but if others thought so they were not to show it. She still hoped, by degrees, to make Dollie a figure easier to deal with at such neighbourly gatherings. She had abandoned any hope that Dollie would grow; anything so feeble and so foolish could not grow; there was no other girl under the little dancer; she was simply no more and no less than she showed herself to be; but, at this later stage of their relationship, Mrs. Bradley essayed, now and then, a deliberate if kindly severity,—as to heels, as to scents, as to touches of rouge.

"Oh, but I'm as careful, just as careful, Mrs. Bradley!" Dollie protested. "I can't walk in lower heels. They hurt my instep. I've a very high instep and it needs support." She was genuinely amazed that any one could dislike her scent and that any one could think the rouge unbecoming. She seemed to acquiesce, but the acquiescence was followed by moods of mournfulness and even by tears. There was no capacity in her for temper or rebellion, and she was all unconscious of giving a warning as she sobbed, "It's nothing—really nothing, Mrs. Bradley. I'm sure you mean to be kind. Only—it's rather quiet and lonely here. I've always been used to so many people,—to having everything so bright and jolly."

She was not rapacious; she was not dissolute; she could be kept respectable and even contented if she were not made too aware of the contrast between her past existence and her present lot. With an air only of pensive pride she would sometimes point out to Mrs. Bradley, in the pages of those same illustrated weeklies with which her mother-in-law associated her, the face of some former companion. One of these young ladies had recently married the son of a peer. "She is in luck, Floss," said Dollie. "We always thought it would come to that. He's been gone on her for ages, but his people were horrid."

Mrs. Bradley felt that, at all events, Dollie had no ground for thinking her "horrid"; yet she imagined that there lay drowsing at the back of her mind a plaintive little sense of being caught and imprisoned. Floss had stepped, triumphant, from the footlights to the registrar's office, and apparently had succeeded in uniting the radiance of her past and present status. No, Dollie could be kept respectable and contented only if the pressure were of the lightest. She could not change, she could only shift; and although Mrs. Bradley felt that for herself, her life behind her, her story told, she could manage to put up with a merely shifted Dollie, she could not see how Jack was to manage it. What was Jack to do with her? was the thought that pressed with a growing weight on her heart. She could never be of Jack's life; yet here she was, in it, planted there by his own generous yet inevitable act, and by hers,—in its very centre, and not to be evaded or forgotten.

And the contrast between what Jack's life might have been and what it now must be was made more poignantly apparent to her when Frances Graham came down to stay from a Saturday to Monday; Frances in her black, tired and thin from Red-Cross work in London; bereaved in more, her old friend knew, than dear Toppie's death; yet with her leisurely, unstressed cheerfulness almost unaltered, the lightness that went with so much tenderness, the drollery that went with so much depth. Dearest, most charming of girls—but for Jack's wretched stumble into "fairyland" last summer, destined obviously to be his wife,—could any presence have shown more disastrously, in its contrast with poor Dollie, how Jack had done for himself? She watched the two together that evening, Frances with her thick crinkled hair and clearly curved brow and her merry, steady eyes, leaning, elbow on knee, to talk and listen to Dollie; and Dollie, poor Dollie, flushed, touched with an unbecoming sulkiness, aware, swiftly and unerringly, of a rival type. Frances was of the type that young men married when they did not "do for themselves." There was now no gulf of age or habit to veil from Dollie her disadvantage. She answered shortly, with now and then a dry, ironic little laugh; and, getting up at last, she went to the piano and loudly played.

"He couldn't have done differently. It was the only thing he could do," Frances said that night before her bedroom fire. She did not hide her recognition of Jack's plight, but she was staunch.

"I wouldn't have had him do differently. But it will ruin his life," said the mother. "If he comes back it will ruin his life."

"No, no," said Frances, looking at the flames. "Why should it? A man doesn't depend on his marriage like that. He has his career."

"Yes. He has his career. A career isn't a life."

"Isn't it?" The girl gazed down. "But it's what so many people have to put up with. And so many haven't even a career." Something came into her voice and she turned from it quickly. "He's crippled, in a sense, of course. But you are here. He will have you to come back to always."

"I shall soon be old, dear, and she will always be here. That's inevitable. Some day I shall have to leave her to Jack to bear with alone."

"She may become more of a companion."

"No; no, she won't." The bitterness of the mother's heart expressed itself in the dry, light utterance. It was a comfort to express bitterness, for once, to somebody.

"She is a harmless little thing," Frances offered after a moment.

"Harmless?" Mrs. Bradley turned it over drily and lightly. "I can't feel her that. I feel her blameless if you like. And it will be easy to keep her contented. That is really the best that one can say of poor Dollie. And then there will be the child. I am pinning all my hopes to the child, Frances."

Frances understood that.

Dollie, as the winter wore on, kept remarkably well. She had felt it the proper thing to allude to Jack and his danger; and so, now, she more and more frequently felt it the proper thing to allude, humorously if with a touch of melancholy, to "baby." Her main interest in baby, Mrs. Bradley felt, was an alarmed one. She was a good deal frightened, poor little soul, and in need of constant reassurances; and it was when one need only pet and pity Dollie that she was easier to deal with. Mrs. Bradley tried to interest her in plans for the baby; what it should be named, and how its hair should be done if it were a little girl,—for only on this assumption could Dollie's interest be at all vividly roused; and Mrs. Bradley more than ever hoped for a boy when she found Dollie's idle yet stubborn thoughts fixed on the name of Gloria.

She was able to evade discussion of this point, and when the baby came, fortunately and robustly, into the world on a fine March morning, she could feel it as a minor but very real cause for thanksgiving that Dollie need now never know what she thought of Gloria as a name. The baby was a boy, and now that he was here Dollie seemed as well pleased that he should be a commonplace Jack, and that there should be no question of tying his hair with cockades of ribbon over each ear. Smiling and rosy and languid, she lay in her charming room, not at all more maternal—though she showed a bland satisfaction in her child and noted that his eyes were just like Jack's—yet subtly more wifely. Baby, she no doubt felt, with the dim instinct that did duty for thought with her, placed and rooted her and gave her final rights. She referred now to Jack with the pensive but open affection of their shared complacency, and made her mother-in-law think, as she lay there, of a soft and sleepy and tenacious creeper, fixing tentacle after tentacle in the walls of Jack's house of life.

If only one could feel that she had furnished it with a treasure! Gravely, with a sad fondness, the grandmother studied the little face, so unfamiliar, for signs of Jack. She was a helplessly clear-sighted woman, and remembrance was poignantly vivid in her of Jack's face at a week old. Already she loved the baby since its eyes, indubitably, were his; but she could find no other trace of him. It was not a Bradley baby; and in the dreamy, foreboding flickers of individuality that pass uncannily across an infant's features, her melancholy and steady discernment could see only the Watson ancestry.

She was to do all she could for the baby; to save him, so far as might be, from his Watson ancestry and to keep him, so far as might be, Jack's and hers. That was to be her task. But with all the moulding that could, mercifully, be applied from the very beginning, she could not bring herself to believe that this was ever to be a very significant human being.

She sent Jack his wire: "A son. Dollie doing splendidly." And she had his answer: "Best thanks. Love to Dollie." It was curious, indeed, this strange new fact they had now, always, to deal with; this light little "Dollie" that must be passed between them. The baby might have made Jack happy, but it had not solved the problem of his future.

III

A WEEK later the telegram was brought to her telling her that he had been killed in action.

It was a beautiful spring day, just such a day as that on which she and Jack had first seen Dorrington, and she had been working in the garden. When she had read, she turned and walked down the path that led to the hazel-copse. She hardly knew what had happened to her; there was only an instinct for flight, concealment, secrecy; but, as she walked, there rose in her, without sound, as if in a nightmare, the terrible cry of her loneliness. The dark wet earth that covered him seemed heaped upon her heart.

The hazel-copse was tasselled thickly with golden-green, and as she entered it she saw that the hepaticas were in flower. They seemed to shine with their own celestial whiteness, set in their melancholy green among the fallen leaves. She had never seen them look so beautiful.

She followed the path, looking down at them, and she seemed to feel Jack's little hand in hers and to see, at her side, his nut-brown head. It had been on just such a morning. She came to the stone bench; but the impulse that had led her here was altered. She did not sink down and cover her face, but stood looking around her at the flowers, the telegram still open in her hand; and slowly, with stealing calm, the sense of sanctuary fell about her.

She had lost him, and with him went all her life. He was dead, his youth and strength and beauty. Yet what was this strange up-welling of relief, deep, deep relief, for Jack; this gladness, poignant and celestial, like that of the hepaticas? He was dead and the dark earth covered him; yet he was here, with her, safe in his youth and strength and beauty, forever. He had died the glorious death, and no future, tangled, perplexed, fretful with its foolish burden, lay before him. There was no loss for Jack; no fading, no waste. The burden was for her and he was free.

Later when pain should have dissolved thought her agony would come to her unalleviated; but this hour was hers and his. She heard the river and the soft whisperings of spring. A bird dropped lightly unafraid from branch to branch of a tree near by. From the woods came the rapid insistent tapping of a woodpecker; and as in so many springs she seemed to hear Jack say, "Hark, mummy," and his little hand was always held in hers. And everywhere telling of irreparable loss, of a possession unalterable, the tragic, the celestial hepaticas.

She sat down on the stone bench now and closed her eyes for a little while so holding them more closely—Jack and the hepaticas—together.

DAFFODILS

I

THOUGH he knew that he was going to die, Marmaduke Follett as he lay in the hospital on the French coast had never in his life been so happy. Until these last days he had not been able to feel it in its completeness. Of the great engagement where he had fallen he remembered only the overwhelming uproar, the blood and mud; and after that, torments, apathies, dim awakenings to the smell of ether and relapses to acquiescent sleep. Now the last operation had failed—or rather, he had failed to recover from it—and there was no more hope for him; but he hardly suffered and his thoughts were emerging into a world of cleanliness, kindness, and repose.

The hospital before the war had been a big hotel, and his was one of the bedrooms on the second floor, its windows crossed by two broad blue bands of sea and sky. As an officer he had a room to himself. The men were in the wards downstairs.

One of his nurses—both were pleasant girls but this was the one who with a wing of black hair curving under her cap reminded him of his cousin Victoria—had put a glass of daffodils beside his bed, not garden daffodils, but the wild ones that grow in woods; and if she made him think of Victoria how much more they made him think of the woods in spring at Channerley!

He was dying after a gallant deed. It was a fitting death for a Follett and so little in his life had been at all fitted to that initial privilege: it was only in the manner of his death that his life matched at all those thoughts of Victoria and Channerley.

He did not remember much of the manner; it still remained cloaked in the overwhelming uproar; but as he lay there he seemed to read in the columns of the London papers what all the Folletts were so soon to read—because of him:—

"His Majesty the King has been graciously pleased to award the Victoria Cross to the under-mentioned officers, non-commissioned officers and men:—

"Sec. Lt. Marmaduke Everard Follett. For most conspicuous bravery.

"He was directed with 50 men to drive the enemy from their trench and under intense shell-and machine-gun fire he personally led three separate parties of bombers against a captured 325 yards of trench; attacking the machine gun, shooting the firer with his revolver, and destroying gun and personnel with bombs. This very brave act saved many lives and ensured the success of the attack. In carrying one of his men back to safety Sec. Lt. Follett was mortally wounded."

He felt himself smile, as he soberly spaced it out, to remember that the youths at the office used to call him Marmalade. It was curious that he most felt his present and his present transfigured self, when he thought of Cauldwell's office, where so many years of his past had been spent. When he thought of that, of the jocund youths, of the weary hours and wasted years, it was to feel himself transfigured; when he thought of the Folletts and of Channerley, to feel that he matched them; to feel at last as if he had come home. What to the grimy, everyday world counted as transfiguration, counted as the normal, the expected, to the world of Channerley.

He wondered, lying there and looking out past the daffodils, where Victoria was; he had heard that she was nursing, too, somewhere in France; and again, as he had smiled over the contrast of "Sec. Lt. Marmaduke Everard Follett" and the "Marmalade" of Cauldwell's office, he smiled in thinking of the difference between Victoria and the nice young nurse who, for all her resembling curve of hair, was also second-rate. It would have been very wonderful to have been nursed by Victoria, and yet his thought turned from that. There had never been any sweetness, never even any kindness for him, in Victoria's clear young gaze; when it came to nursing, he could imagine her being kind to a Tommy, but not to him, the dull, submerged cousin; and the nice though second-rate nurse was very kind. He would rather die under her eyes than under Victoria's.

And he would rather think of Victoria as he had last seen her at the big London dance to which, most unexpectedly, he had found himself asked last spring—the spring before the war. He had decided, as with nervous fingers he tied his white cravat,—how rarely disturbed had been that neat sheaf lying in his upper drawer!—that he must have been confused with some other Follett, for he was so seldom asked anywhere, where he would be likely to meet Victoria. However, it was a delight to see her in her snowy dress, her beautiful hair bound with silver, and to feel, as he watched her dancing, that she belonged, in a sense, to him; for he, too, was a Follett.

How much more did she belong to him now! And not only Victoria, but all of them, these Folletts of his and the Folletts of past generations; and Channerley, centre of all his aching, wistful memories. It had been for him, always, part of the very structure of his nature, that beautiful old house where he had spent his boyhood. Perhaps it was because he had been turned out of the nest so early that he never ceased to miss it. His thought, like a maimed fledgling, had fluttered round and round it, longing, exiled, helpless.

If, now, he could have survived, his eldest brother, he felt sure, must have asked him oftener to stay at Channerley. It still gave him a pang, or, rather, the memory of many pangs, to recall that Robert had not asked him for two years, and had seemed to forget all about him after that. They had all seemed to forget about him,—that was the trouble of it,—and almost from the very beginning: Robert, who had Channerley; Austin, who had gone into the army and was now in Mesopotamia; Griselda, married so splendidly up in her northern estate; and Amy, the artistic bachelor-girl of the family, whom he associated with irony and cigarette-smoke and prolonged absences in Paris. Even cheerful Sylvia, of South Kensington, with her many babies and K.C. husband, whom he always thought of, for all her well-being, as very nearly as submerged as himself,—even Sylvia saw little of him and asked him only to family dinners,—Mr. Shillington's family, not hers,—at depressingly punctual intervals.

But Sylvia, the one nearest him in years, was the one who had forgotten least, and she had, after her fashion, done her best for him. Confused at study, clumsy at games, shy and tongue-tied, he had not in any way distinguished himself at a rather second-rate public school; and to distinguish himself had been the only hope for him. The Folletts had never had any money to spare, and Eton and Oxford for Robert and Sandhurst for Austin fulfilled a tradition that became detached and terse where younger sons who could not distinguish themselves were concerned. Still, he had always felt that, had his father lived, something better would have been found for him than to be bundled, through the instrumentality of Mr. Shillington, into a solicitor's office. There he had been bundled, and there he had stuck for all these years, as clumsy, as confused as ever; a pallid, insignificant little fellow (oh, he had no illusions about himself!) with the yellow hair and small yellow moustache which, together with his name, had earned for him his sobriquet.

They had not disliked him, those direfully facetious companions of his. Noblesse oblige was an integral part of his conception of himself, however little they might be aware of his unvarying courtesy towards them as its exercise. He suspected that they thought of him as merely inoffensive and rather piteous; but shyness might give that impression; they could not guess at the quiet aversion that it covered. He was aware sometimes, suddenly, that in the aloofness and contemplative disdain of his pale sidelong glance at them, he most felt himself a Follett. If his mind, for most practical purposes, was slow and clumsy, it was sharp and swift in its perceptions. He judged the young men in Cauldwell's office as a Follett must judge them. In the accurate applying of that standard he was as instinctively gifted as any of his race; and if he knew, from his first look at her, that the nice young nurse was second-rate, how coldly and calmly, all these years, he had known that the young men who called him Marmalade were third-rate. And yet they none of them disliked him, and he wondered whether it was because, when he most felt disdain, he most looked merely timid, or because they recognized in him, all dimly as it might be, the first-rateness that was his inherently and inalienably.

Just as the third-rate young men might recognize the first-rate but dimly, he was aware that to the world the Folletts, too, were not important. It was not one of the names, in spite of centuries of local lustre, to conjure with; and he liked it all the better because of that. They had never, it was true, distinguished themselves; but they were people of distinction, and that was, to his quiet, reflective, savouring, an even higher state. He sometimes wondered if, in any of them, the centring of family consciousness was as intense as in himself. If they were aloof about third-rate people, it was not because they were really very conscious about themselves. They took themselves for granted, as they took Channerley and the family history; and only Amy was aware that some of the family portraits were good.

The history—it was not of course accurate to call it that, yet it seemed more spacious and significant than mere annals—pored over during long evenings, in faded parchments, deeds, and letters, was known in every least detail to him. How the Folletts had begun, very soberly but very decorously, in the fifteenth century, and how they had gone on: rooting more deeply into their pleasant woodlands and meadows; flowering, down the centuries, now in a type of grace—that charming Antonia who had married so well at James the First's court; and of gallantry—a Follett had fallen at Naseby, and a Follett had fought at Waterloo; or of good-humoured efficiency, as in the eighteenth-century judge and the nineteenth-century bishop. And he, who was neither graceful nor gallant nor good-humoured (sour and sad he felt himself), never could resist the warming, revivifying influence of these recognitions, stretching himself, sighing, smiling happily before his Bloomsbury fire on a winter's evening, as he laid down the thick pile of yellowed manuscripts to think it all over and feel himself, in spite of everything, a link with it all.

Robert had always been very decent about letting him have and keep the documents for as long as he liked.

It was strange to think that he was never to see his Bloomsbury lodgings again, and stranger, really, that a certain tinge of regret was in the thought;

for how, for years, he had hated them, place of exile, of relegation, as he had always felt them! Yet he had come to be fond of his little sitting-room, just because, to his eye, with its mingled comfort and austerity, it was so significant of exile. If a Follett couldn't have what he wanted, that was all he would have—his rack of pipes, his shelves of books, his little collection of mostly marginless mezzotints ranged along the dark, green walls. The room was a refuge and did not pretend to be an achievement, and in that very fact might, to an eye as sharp as his for such significance, suggest the tastes that it relinquished. He had indeed all the tastes and none of the satisfactions of Channerley.

There it was; he had come back to it again, as, indeed, he had, in spirit, never left it—never for a moment. He felt himself, lying there in the hospital on the French coast, with the soft spring sea lapping upon the beach under his window—he felt himself drop, drop, softly, sweetly, deeply, back to his childhood. From his high nursery-window he saw the dewy tree-tops,—the old hawthorn that grew so near the house, and the old mulberry,—and the rooks wheeling on a spring sky so many years ago. The dogs, at that early hour, just released, might be racing over the lawns: idle, jovial Peter, the spaniel, and Jack, the plucky, hot-tempered little Dandy-Dinmont.

Below the lawns were the high grey garden walls, and above, rising a little from the flagged rose-garden, were the woods where the daffodils grew, daffodils like those beside him now, tall and small, their pale, bright pennons set among warrior spears of green. Little bands of them ran out upon the lawn from under the great trees, and one saw their gold glimmering far, far along the woodlands. Oh, the beauty of it, and the stillness; the age and youth; the smile and the security! How he had always loved it, shambling about the woods and gardens; creeping rather—he always saw himself as creeping somehow—about the dear, gay, faded house! Always such an awkward, insignificant little boy; even his dear old Nanna had felt dissatisfied with his appearance, and he had always known it, when she sent him down with the others to the drawing-room; and his mother, she had made it very apparent, had found him only that.

He shrank from the thought of his mother; perhaps it was because of her, of her vexed and averted eyes, her silken rustle of indifference as she passed him by, that he saw himself as creeping anywhere where she might come. He only remembered her in glimpses: languidly and ironically smiling at her tea-table (Amy had her smile), the artificial tone of her voice had even then struck his boyish ear; reading on a summer afternoon, with bored brows and dissatisfied lips, as she lay on a garden chair in the shade of the mulberry tree; querulously arguing with his father, who, good-humoured and very indifferent, strolled about the hall in his pink coat on a winter morning, waiting for the horses to be brought round; his mother's yellow braids shining under her neatly tilted riding-hat, her booted foot held to the blaze of the great log-fire. A hard, selfish, sentimental woman; and—wasn't it really the only word for what he felt in her?—just a little shoddy. He distinguished it from the second-rate nicely: it was a more personal matter; for his mother, though certainly not a Follett, was of good stock; he knew, of course, all about her stock. It always grieved him to think that it was from her he had his yellow hair and the pale grey of his eyes; his stature, too, for she had been a small woman; all the other Folletts were tall; but she had given him nothing more: not a trace of her beauty was his, and he was glad of it.

It was curious, since he had really had so little to do with him, as little, almost, as with his mother, how blissfully his sense of his father's presence pervaded his childish memories. He was so kind. The kindest thing he remembered at Channerley, except his dear old Nanna and Peter the spaniel. It used to give him a thrill of purest joy when, meeting him, his father, his hands clasped behind his back after his strolling wont, would stop and bend amused and affectionate eyes upon him; rather the eyes, to be sure, that he bent upon his dogs; but Marmaduke always felt of him that he looked upon his children, and upon himself, too, as parts of the pack; and it was delightful to be one of the pack, with him.

"Well, old fellow, and how goes the world with you to-day?" his father would say.

And after that question the world would go in sunshine.

He had always believed that, had his father lived, he would never have been so forgotten; just as he had always believed that his father would never have allowed one of his pack to be bundled into the solicitor's office. For that he had to thank, he felt sure, not only Sylvia's negative solicitude, but his mother's active indifference. Between them both they had done it to him.

And he never felt so to the full his dispossession as in thinking of Robert. He had always intensely feared and admired Robert. He did not know what he feared, for Robert was never unkind. But Robert was everything that he was not: tall and gay and competent, and possessing everything needful, from the very beginning, for the perfect fulfilment of his type. The difference between them had been far more than the ten years that had made of Robert a man when he was still only a little boy. There had been, after all, a time when they had been a very big and a very little boy together, with Austin in between; yet the link had seemed always to break down after Austin. Robert, in this retrospect, had always the air of strolling away from him—for Robert, too, was a stroller. Not that he himself had had the air of pursuit; he had never, he felt sure, from the earliest age, lacked tact; tact and reticence and self-effacement had been bred into him. But his relationship with Robert had seemed always to consist in standing there, hiding ruefulness, and gazing at Robert's strolling back.

The difference from Austin had perhaps been as great, but it had never hurt so much, for Austin, though with his share of the Follett charm, had never had the charm of Robert. A clear-voiced and clear-eyed, masterful boy, Austin's main contact with others was in doing things with them, and that sort of contact did not mean congeniality. Austin had made use of him; had let him hold his ferrets and field for him at cricket; and a person whom you found useful did not, for the time being, bore you.

But he had bored Robert always—that was apparent; and beautiful Griselda, who was older than either of them, and Amy, who was younger. Griselda had gazed rather sadly over his head; and Amy had smiled and teased him so that he had seldom ventured on a remark in her presence. Even fat little Sylvia, the baby, had always preferred any of the others to him as she grew up; had only not been bored because, while she was good-humoured, she was also rather dull. And at the bottom of his heart, rueful always, sore, and still patiently surprised, he knew that, while he found them all a little brutal, he could not admire them the less because of it. It was part of the Follett inheritance to be able to be brutal, unconsciously, and therefore with no loss of bloom.

And now, at last, he was not to bore them any longer; at last, he was not to be forgotten. How could he not be happy,—it brought back every blissful thrill of boyhood, his father's smile, the daffodil woods in spring, heightened to ecstasy,—when he had at last made of himself one of the Folletts who were remembered? He would have his place in the history beside the Follett who fell at Naseby. No family but is glad of a V.C. in its annals. They could no longer stroll away. They would be proud of him; he had done something for all the Folletts forever.

II

THE nice young nurse came in. She closed the door gently, and, with her smile, calm before accustomed death, and always, as it were, a little proud of him,—that was because they were both English,—she took his wrist and felt his pulse, holding her watch in the other hand, and asked him, presently, how he felt. Only after that did she say, contemplating him for a moment,—Marmaduke wondered how many hours—or was it perhaps days?—she was giving him to live,—

"A gentleman has come to see you. You may see him if you like. But I've told him that he is only to stay for half an hour."

The blood flowed up to Marmaduke's forehead. He felt it beating hard in his neck and behind his ears, and his heart thumped down there under the neatly drawn bed-clothes.

"A gentleman? What's his name?"

Was it Robert?

"Here is his card," said the nurse.

She drew it from her pocket and gave it to him. It couldn't have been Robert, of course. Robert would only have had to come up. Yet he was dizzy with the disappointment. It was as if he saw Robert strolling away for the last time. He would never see Robert again.

Mr. Guy Thorpe was the name. The address was a London club that Marmaduke placed at once as second-rate, and "The Beeches, Arlington Road," in a London suburb. On the card was written in a neat scholarly hand: "May I see you? We are friends."

It was difficult for a moment to feel anything but the receding tide of his hope. The next thing that came was a sense of dislike for Mr. Guy Thorpe and for the words that he had written. Friends? By what right since he did not know his name?

"Is he a soldier?" he asked. "How did he come? I don't know him."

"You needn't see him unless you want to," said the nurse. "No; he's not a soldier. An elderly man. He's driving a motor for the French Wounded Emergency Fund, and came on from the Alliance because he heard that you were here. Perhaps he's some old family friend. He spoke as if he were."

Marmaduke smiled a little. "That's hardly likely. But I'll see him, yes; since he came for that."

When she had gone, he lay looking again at the blue bands across the window. A flock of sea-gulls flew past—proud, swift, and leisurely, glittering in the sun. They seemed to embody the splendour and exultation of his thoughts, and, when they had disappeared, he was sorry, almost desolate.

Mr. Guy Thorpe. He took up the card again in his feeble hand and looked at it. And now, dimly, it seemed to remind him of something.

Steps approached along the passage, the nurse's light footfall and the heavier, careful tread of a man. An oddly polite, almost a deprecating tread. He had gone about a great many hospitals and was cautious not to disturb wounded men. Yet Marmaduke felt again that he did not like Mr. Guy Thorpe, and, as they came in, he was conscious of feeling a little frightened.

There was nothing to frighten one in Mr. Thorpe's appearance. He was a tall, thin, ageing man, travel-worn, in civilian clothes, with a dingy Red-Cross badge on the sleeve of his waterproof overcoat. Baldish and apparently near-sighted, he seemed to blink towards the bed, and, as if with motoring in the wind, his eyelids were moist and reddened. He sat down, murmuring some words of thanks to the nurse.

A very insignificant man, for all his height and his big forehead. Altogether of The Beeches, Arlington Road. Had he turned grey, he might have looked less shabby, but dark thin locks still clustered above his high crown and behind his long-lobed ears. His eyes were dark, his moustache drooped, and he had a small, straight nose. Marmaduke saw that he was the sort of man who, in youth, might have been considered very handsome. He looked like a seedy poet and some sort of minor civil servant mingled, the civil servant having got the better of the poet. Marmaduke also imagined that he would have a large family and a harassed but ambitious wife, with a genteel accent—a wife a little below himself. His tie was of a dull red silk. Marmaduke did not like him.

Mr. Thorpe glanced round, as if cautiously, to see if the nurse had closed the door, and then, it was really as if more cautiously still, looked at Marmaduke, slightly moving back his chair.

"I'm very grateful to you, very grateful indeed," he said in a low voice, "for seeing me."

"You've come a long way," said Marmaduke.

"Yes. A long way. I had heard of your being here. I hoped to get here. I felt that I must see you. We are all proud of you; more proud than I can say."

He looked down now at the motoring-cap he held, and Marmaduke became aware that the reddened eyes were still more suffused and that the mouth under the drooping moustache twitched and trembled. He could think of nothing to say, except to murmur something about being very glad—though he didn't want to say that; and he supposed, to account for Mr. Thorpe's emotion, that he must be a moving sight, lying there, wasted, bandaged, and dying.

"You don't remember my name, I suppose," said Mr. Thorpe after a moment, in which he frankly got out his handkerchief and wiped his eyes.

"No, I'm afraid I don't," said Marmaduke very politely. He was glad to say this. It was the sort of thing he did want to say.

"Yet I know yours very, very well," said Mr. Thorpe, with a curious watery smile. "I lived at Channerley once. I was tutor there for some time—to Robert, your brother, and Griselda. Yes," Mr. Thorpe nodded, "I know the Folletts well; and Channerley, the dear old place."

Now the dim something in memory pressed forward, almost with a physical advance, and revealed itself as sundry words scratched on the schoolroom window-panes and sundry succinct drawings in battered old Greek and Latin grammars. Robert had always been very clever at drawing, catching with equal facility and accuracy the swiftness of a galloping horse and the absurdities of a human profile. What returned to Marmaduke now, and as clearly as if he had the fly-leaf before him, was a tiny thumb-nail sketch of such a galloping horse unseating a lank, crouching figure, of whom the main indications were the angles of acute uncertainty taken by the knees and elbows; and a more elaborate portrait, dashed and dotted as if with a ruthless boyish grin—such an erect and melancholy head it was, so dark the tossed-back locks, so classical the nose and unclassical the moustache, and a brooding eye indicated in a triangular sweep of shadow. Beneath was written in Robert's clear, boyish hand, "Mr. Guy Thorpe, Poet, Philosopher, and Friend. Vale." Even the date flashed before him, 1880; and with it—strange, inappropriate association—the daffodils running out upon the lawn, as no doubt he had seen them as he leaned from the schoolroom window, with the Greek grammar under his elbow on the sill.

So that was it. Mr. Guy Thorpe, placed, explained, disposed of—poor dear! He felt suddenly quite kindly towards him, quite touched by his act of loyalty to the old allegiance in coming; and flattered, too,—yes, even by Mr.

Thorpe,—that he should be recognized as a Follett who had done something for the name; and smiling very benevolently upon him, he said:—

"Oh, of course; I remember perfectly now—your name, and drawings of you in old schoolbooks, you know. All tutors and governesses get those tributes from their pupils, don't they? But I myself couldn't remember, could I? for it was before I was born that you were at Channerley."

There was a moment of silence after this, and in it Marmaduke felt that Mr. Thorpe did not like being so placed. He had no doubt imagined that there would be less ambiguous tributes, and that his old pupils would have talked of him to the younger generation.

And something of this chagrin certainly came out in his next words as, nodding and looking round at the daffodils, he said:—

"Yes, yes. Quite true. No, of course you couldn't yourself remember. I was more though, I think I may fairly say, than the usual tutor or governess. I came, rather, at Sir Robert's instance."—Sir Robert was Marmaduke's father.—"We had met, made friends, at Oxford; his former tutor there was an uncle of mine, and Sir Robert, in my undergraduate days, used to visit him sometimes. He was very keen on getting me to come. Young Robert wanted something of a firm hand. I was the friend rather than the mere man of books in the family."

"Poet, Philosopher and Friend"—Marmaduke had it almost on his lips, and almost with a laugh, his benevolence deepened for poor Mr. Thorpe, so self-revealed, so entirely Robert's portrait of him. Amusing to think that even the quite immature first-rate can so relegate the third. But perhaps it was a little unfair to call poor Mr. Thorpe third. The Folletts would not be likely to choose a third-rate man for a tutor; second was kinder, and truer. He had, obviously, come down in the world.

"I see. It's natural I never heard, though: there's such a chasm between the elders and the youngers in a big family, isn't there?" he said. "Griselda is twelve years older than I am, and Robert ten, you remember. She was married by the time I began my Greek. You never came back to Channerley, did you? I hope things have gone well with you since those days?"

He questioned, wanting to be very kind; wanting to give something of the genial impression of his father smiling, with his "And how goes the world with you to-day?" But he saw that, while Mr. Thorpe's evident emotion deepened, it was with a sense of present grief as well as of retrospective pathos.

"No; I never came,—that is—. No; I passed by: I never came to stay. I went abroad; I travelled, with a pupil, for some years before my marriage." Grief and confusion were oddly mingled in his drooping face. "And after that—life had changed too much. My dear old friend Sir Robert had died. I could not have faced it all. No, no; when some chapters are read, it is better to close the book; better to close the book. But I have never forgotten Channerley, nor the Folletts of Channerley; that will always remain for me the golden page; the page," said Mr. Thorpe, glancing round again at the daffodils, "of friendship, of youth, of daffodils in springtime. I saw you there," he added suddenly, "once, when you were a very little lad. I saw you. I was passing by; bicycling; no time to stop. You remember the high road skirts the woods to the north. I came and looked over the wall; and there you were—in your holland pinafore and white socks—digging up the daffodils and putting them into your little red-and-yellow cart. A beautiful spring morning. The woods full of sunshine. You wouldn't remember."

But he did remember—perfectly. Not having been seen; but the day; the woods; the daffodils. He had dug them up to plant in his own little garden, down below. He had always been stupid with his garden; had always failed where the other succeeded. And he had wanted to be sure of daffodils. And they had all laughed at him for wanting the wild daffodils like that for himself, and for going to get them in the wood. And why had Mr. Thorpe looked over the wall and not come in? He hated to think that he had been watched on that spring morning—hated it. And, curiously, that sense of fear with which he had heard the approaching footsteps returned to him. It frightened him that Mr. Thorpe had watched him over the wall.

His distaste and shrinking were perhaps apparent in his face, for it was with a change of tone and hastiness of utterance, as though hurrying away from something, that Mr. Thorpe went on:— "You see,—it's been my romance, always, Channerley—and all of you. I've always followed your lives—always—from a distance—known what you were up to. I've made excuses to myself—in the days when I used to go a good deal about the country—to pass by Channerley and just have a glimpse of you. And when I heard that you had done this noble deed,—when I heard what you had done for England, for Channerley, for us all,—I felt I had to come and see you. You must forgive me if I seem a mere intruder. I can't seem that to myself. I've cared too much. And what I came for, really, was to thank you,—to thank you, my dear boy,—and to tell you that because of you, life must be nobler, always, for all of us."

His words had effaced the silly, groping fear. It was indeed, since his colonel's visit, the first congratulation he had had from the outer world. The nurses, of course, had congratulated him, and the surgeons; but no one who knew him outside; the kindly telegrams from Robert and Sylvia did not count as congratulations. And in a way poor Mr. Thorpe did know him, and though it was only from him, it had its sweetness. He felt himself flush as he answered, "That's very kind of you."

"Oh, no!" said Mr. Thorpe, shaking his head and swinging his foot—Marmaduke knew that from the queer movement of his body as he sat with very tightly folded arms. "Not kind! That's not the word—from us to you! Not the word at all!"

"I'm very happy, as you may imagine," said Marmaduke. And he was happy again, and glad to share his happiness with poor Mr. Thorpe. "It makes everything worth while, doesn't it, to have brought it off at all?"

"Everything, everything—it would; it would, to you. So heroes feel," said Mr. Thorpe. "To give your life for England. I know it all—in every detail. Yes, you are happy in dying that England may live. Brave boy! Splendid boy!"

Now he was weeping. He had out his handkerchief and his shoulders shook. It made Marmaduke want to cry, too, and he wondered confusedly if the nurse would soon come back. Had not the half hour passed?

"Really—it's too good of you. You mustn't, you know; you mustn't," he murmured, while the word, "boy—boy," repeated, made tangled images in his mind, and he saw himself in the white socks and with the little red-and-yellow cart, and then as he had been the other day, leading his men, his revolver in his hand and the bullets flying about him. "And I'm not a boy," he said; "I'm thirty-four; absurdly old to be only a second lieutenant. And there are so many of us. Why,"—the thought came fantastically, but he seized it, because Mr. Thorpe was crying so and he must seize something,—"we're as common as daffodils!"

"Ah! not for me! not for me!" Mr. Thorpe gulped quickly. Something had given way in him—as if the word "daffodils" had pressed a spring. He was sobbing aloud, and he had fallen on his knees by the bed and put up his hand for Marmaduke's. "I cannot keep it from you! Not at this last hour! Not when you are leaving me forever!—My son! My brave son! I am your father, Marmaduke! I am your father, my dear, dear boy!"

III

IT was the stillest room. The two calm bands of blue crossed the window. In the sunlight the gulls came flying back. Marmaduke looked out at them. Were they the same sea-gulls or another flock? Then quietly he closed his eyes. Stillness—calm. But something else was rising to him from them. Darkness; darkness; a darkness worse than death. Oh! death was sweet compared to this. Compared to this all his life had been sweet; and something far dearer than life was being taken from him. He only knew the terrible confusion of his whole nature.

He opened his eyes again with an instinct of escape. There were the bands of blue, and, still passing in their multitudes, leaving him forever, the proud, exultant sea-gulls. The man still knelt beside him. He heard his own voice come:—

"What do you mean?"

"I never meant to tell you! I never meant to tell you!" a moan answered him. "But—seeing you lying there!—dying!—my son!—who has given his life for England!—And how I have longed for you all these years!—My romance, Marmaduke—How could I be silent? Forgive me! Forgive me, my boy. Yes, mine. My known children are dear to me, but how far dearer the unknown son, seen only by stealth, in snatched glimpses! It is true, Marmaduke, true. We were lovers. She loved me. Do not ask. Do not question. We were young. She was very beautiful. It was springtime; daffodils were in the woods. She said that she had never known any one like me. She said that her life was hollow, meaningless. I opened doors to her, I read to her. Browning—I read Browning," he muttered on, "in the woods; among the daffodils. It was a new life to her—and to me. And we were swept away. Don't blame us, Marmaduke. If there was wrong, there was great beauty—then. Only then; for after, she was cruel—very cruel. She turned from me; she crushed and tore my heart. Oh!—I have suffered! But no one knew. No one ever dreamed of it. Only she and I. My God!—I see her in your hair and eyes!"

It was true. It was absolutely true. Through his whole being he felt its inevitability. Everything was clear, with a strange, black, infernal clearness. His life lay open before him, open from beginning to end: that beginning of tawdry sentiment and shame—with daffodils; and this end, with daffodils again, and again with tawdry sentiment and shame.

He was not a Follett. He had no part in the Folletts. He had no part in Channerley. He was an interloper, a thief. He was the son of this wretched man, in whose very grief he could detect the satisfaction—oh, who more fitted to detect such satisfaction!—of his claim upon a status above his own. He was all that he had always most despised, a second-rate, a third-rate little creature; the anxious, civil, shrinking Marmalade of Cauldwell's office. Why (as the hideous moments led him on, point by point, his old lucidity, sharpened to a needle fineness, seemed to etch the truth in lines of fire upon the blackness), hadn't he always been a pitiful little snob? Wasn't it of the essence of a snob to over-value the things one hadn't and to fear the things one was? It hadn't been other people, it had been himself, what he really was, of whom he had always been afraid. He saw himself reduced to the heretofore unrecognized, yet always operative, element in his own nature—a timid, watchful humility.

Oh, Channerley! Channerley! The wail rose in his heart and it filled the world. Oh, his woods, his daffodils, his father's smile—gone—lost forever! Worse than that—smirched, withered, desecrated!

A hideous gibbering of laughter seemed to rise around him, and pointing fingers. Amy's eyes passed with another malice in their mockery; and Robert would never turn to him now, and Griselda would never look at him. He saw it all, as they would never see it. He was not one of them, and they had always felt it; and oh,—above all,—he had always felt it. And now, quite close it seemed, softly rustling, falsely smiling, moved his loathsome mother: not only as he remembered her in youth, but in her elegant middle years, as he had last seen her, with hard eyes and alien lips and air of brittle, untouched exquisiteness.

Suddenly fury so mounted in him that he saw himself rising in bed, rending his dressings, to seize the kneeling man by the throat and throttle him. He could see his fingers sinking in on either side among the clustered hair, and hear himself say, "How dare you! How dare you! You hound! You snivelling, sneaking hound! You look for pity from me, do you!—and tenderness! Well, take this, this! Everything, everything I am and have that's worth being and having, I owe to them. I've hated you and all you mean, always—yes, your fear and your caution and your admiration and your great high forehead. Oh, I see it! I see it!—it's my own! And though I am only that in myself, then take it from me that I hate myself along with you and curse myself with you!"

It came to him that he was slowly panting, and that after the fever-fury an icy chill crept over him. And a slow, cold smile came with it, and he saw Jephson, the wit of the office, wagging his head and saying, "Little Marmalade take a man by the throat! Ask me another!"

No; little Marmalade might win the V.C.; but only when he thought he was a Follett. Was that what it all came to, really? Something broke and stopped in his mind.

He heard his father's voice. How long ago it had all happened. He had known for years, hadn't he, that this was his father?

"Marmaduke! Mr. Follett! What have I done? Shall I call somebody? Oh, forgive me!"

His father was standing now beside him and bending over him. He looked up at him and shook his head. He did not want any one to come.

"Oh, what have I done?" the man repeated.

"I was dying anyway, you know," he heard himself say.

What a pitiful face it was, this weary, loosened, futureless old face above him! What a frightened face! What long years of slow disgarnishing lay behind it: youth, romance, high hopes, all dropped away. He had come to-day with their last vestiges, still the sentimental, romancing fool, self-centred and craving; but nothing of that was left. He was beaten, at last, down into the very ground. It was a haggard, humiliated, frightened face, and miserable. As he himself had been. But not even death lay before this face. For how many years must it go on sinking down until the earth covered it? Marmaduke seemed to understand all about him, as well as if he had been himself.

"Sit down," he said. He heard that his voice was gentle, though he was not aware of feeling anything, only of understanding. "I was rather upset. No; I don't want any one. Of course I forgive you. Don't bother about it, I beg."

His father sat down, keeping his swollen eyes on the motoring-cap which, unseeingly, he turned and turned in his hands.

"Tell me about yourself a little," said Marmaduke, with slow, spaced breaths. "Where do you live? How? Are you fairly happy?"

He knew that he was not happy; but he might, like most people with whom life had not succeeded, often imagine himself so, and Marmaduke wanted to help him, if possible, to imagine it.

"I live near London. I used to do a good deal of University Extension lecturing. I've a clerkship in the Education Office now." Mr. Thorpe spoke in a dead obedient voice. "A small salary, not much hope of advance; and I've a large family. It's rather up-hill, of course. But I've good children; clever children. My eldest boy's at Oxford; he took a scholarship at Westminster; and my eldest girl's at Girton. The second girl, Winnie, has a very marked gift for painting; she is our artist; we're going to send her to the Slade next year when she leaves the High School. Good children. I've nothing to complain of."

"So you're fairly happy?" Marmaduke repeated. Oddly, he felt himself comforted in hearing about the good and happy children, in hearing about Winnie, her father's favourite.

"Happy? Well, just now, with this terrible war, one can't be that, can one? It is a great adventure for me, however, this work of mine, motoring about France. I don't think I've ever done anything I cared so much about since—for years," said Mr. Thorpe. "It's a beautiful country, isn't it? and the soldiers are such splendid fellows! One gets a lot out of it. But happy? No, I don't suppose I am. I'm pretty much of a failure, and I started life with great imaginings about myself. One doesn't get over that sort of disappointment; one never really gets over it in a way." Mr. Thorpe was looking at him now, and it was as if there were a kindliness between them. "Things have been rather grey and disagreeable on the whole," he said.

"They can be very grey and disagreeable, can't they?" said Marmaduke, closing his eyes.

He was very tired, and as he lay there quietly, having nothing further to know or to suffer, having reached the very limits of conscious dissolution, something else began to come to him. It seemed born of the abolition of self and of the acceptance of the fact that he was dead to all that had given life worth or beauty. It would have been very good to be a Follett; though, he saw it now, he had over-prized that special sort of goodness—with so much else from which he had been, as really, shut out; but he was not a Follett; nor was he merely this poor, insignificant father. He did not quite make out in what the difference lay and he did not rejoice in it, for there was no rejoicing left in him. But, even if the difference were only an acquired instinct (dimly, the terms of his complacent readings in biology and sociology returned to him), even if it were only that, not anything inherent and transmissible, it was, all the same, his own possession; something that he and the Folletts had made together; so that it was as true to say that he had won the V.C. as to say that they had. The lessened self that was left to him had still its worth. To see the truth, even if it undid you, was worthy; to see so unwaveringly that it was good to be a Follett even when you weren't one, had the elements of magnanimity; and to accept the fact of being second-rate proved, did it not?—if you still cared to prove it; he felt himself smile as gently at the relinquished self as he had smiled at his father,—that you were not merely second-rate.

There was now a sound of stumbling movement; doors opening and shutting; nurses, surgeons in the room; and his father's face, far away, against the blue bands, looking at him, still so frightened and so miserable that he tried again to smile at him and to say, "It's all right. Quite all right."

At all events he had been decent to the poor old fellow. His thoughts came brokenly, but he was still seeing something, finding something; it was like a soft light growing. At all events, he had behaved as a Follett would wish to behave even when brought to such a pass. No—but it wasn't quite that, either; it was something new. He had behaved as any one decent should wish to behave. And the daffodils glimmering to his vision seemed to light him further still. "We are as common as daffodils," came back to him. Daffodils were for everybody. Foolish little boy who, on the distant spring morning in the woods of Channerley, dug them up to take them to his own garden!

He was there among them with his little red-and-yellow cart, and the thrush was singing high above him, in the rosy topmost branches of an elm.

Beautiful woods. Beautiful flowers of light and chivalry. How the sunshine streamed among them!

"Dear Channerley," he thought. For again he seemed to belong there.

Gentle hands were tending him and, as he turned his cheek on the pillow, it was with the comfort—almost that of the little boy at Channerley being tucked up in the warm nursery to go to sleep—of knowing that he was dying, and that, in spite of everything, he had given something to the name.

www.ingramcontent.com/pod-product-compliance
Lightning Source LLC
Chambersburg PA
CBHW081729100526
44591CB00016B/2558